IT'S NOT TOO LATE
TO TURN BACK NOW

Back To The Open Arms Of God

EDDIE L. CORNELIUS
With Teena Morena

6 "Seek the Lord while he may be found;

call upon him while he is near;

7 let the wicked forsake his way,

and the unrighteous man his thoughts;

let him return to the Lord, that he may have compassion on him,

and to our God, for he will abundantly pardon.

Isaiah 55:6- 7 (MSG)

That is why the Lord says,

"Turn to me now, while there is time"

Joel 2:12 (NLT)

However, there is also this; it's not too late-

God's personal Message!

"Come back to me and really mean it!

Come fasting and weeping, sorry for your sins!"

Joel 2:12 (MSG)

TABLE OF CONTENTS

PREFACE

Some shows I love to watch on television are those that give you information on celebrities from the past and where they are today. It is the celebrities we grew up watching on our favorite TV shows or possibly the singer who sang our favorite song back in the day.

Those updated stories are sweet to watch, especially when the person is doing rather well in their life outside of the limelight. Of course, you do have those sad stories where the celebrity is not doing so well, and it can make you wish you never heard anything at all.

Searching out information is a risk, after all, curiosity did kill the cat. If we don't know what happened, we can at least assume or imagine the best and move on.

Think about some of the well-known characters in the fairy tales of old. For example, most of us have heard about Cinderella. We know Cinderella married her Prince Charming and that they lived happily ever after. Well, at least that is the last thing we heard about the story.

Pretend for a moment that Cinderella is real and not just a fairy tale character. I would be curious to know a few things about her incredible life. If I could ask her a few questions, I would indeed ask, "How did you feel after marrying a prince? I would ask her if she and her prince had any children together or whatever happened to those evil stepsisters of hers. I would want to know if living in a big castle was all she had hoped it would be.

Maybe I am amongst a small group of people that think like this, but I know that some people may have wondered, "Whatever happened to that 70s group Cornelius Brothers and Sister Rose?" It was an idea that I believe may have crossed the mind of the late Dick Clark and the producers of a 2002 commercial ad for Office Depot. Let me give you a brief description of that commercial ad.

The commercial showed two people on an elevator trying to determine who sang the song that was playing in the background. The song chosen was none other than Too Late to Turn Back Now. Neither of the two people could guess the right artist name, and that was when the late producer mogul Dick Clark came to the scene. He told them the correct title of the song, the recorded year, and the name of the group who performed the song.

The commercial was pointing out the musical expertise of the late Dick Clark. It was drawing a parallel reference to Office Depot being the expert for knowing office supplies.

When I saw the commercial, I was shocked!" I could not believe that out of all the songs ever made, the producer picked Too Late to Turn Back Now. It was the 1972 top hit release from Cornelius Brothers and Sister Rose. Ironically, this was also the year of the song's 30th Anniversary.

Once again, in 2004, the blockbuster movie Anchorman used Treat Her Like a Lady as the opening song. I remember family and friends calling and asking me, "Hey, did you see the new movie Anchorman? "Your dad's song is in the introduction!" Naturally, I decided to watch the movie just to see the intro. It turns out the movie played a good length of the song, not to mention, the film was quite hilarious.

Still yet again, in 2010, one of their songs got airplay on the hit Fox show American Idol. My mouth dropped when I heard idol finalist Lee Dewyze revamp Treat Her Like a Lady. He performed it so masterfully that the judges and audience were quite impressed. They called it his best performance of that round. That was the third time a song by the group had been played on a major platform.

More recently, you can see the song, *Too Late to Turn Back Now,* in a dance scene of Spike Lee's Oscar-nominated movie BlacKkKlansman. The film is based on the true story of a black detective named Ron Stallworth who went undercover as a KKK member. This happened during the 70s so if you lived during those times, you could experience a sense of nostalgia watching the movie.

I was mesmerized by seeing the actors dressed in bell-bottoms, rocking afros, and platform shoes while singing and dancing to a song by the Cornelius Brothers and Sister Rose.

This gave me the idea that maybe people who think like me would want to know, "Whatever happened to that group?" Well, in this book, you will learn that, but you are in store for even more. I invite you to read a fantastic testimony of one of the groups' lead singers and songwriters, Mr. Eddie Cornelius. He sang & wrote the group's most famous songs, including Treat Her Like a Lady and Too Late To Turn Back Now.

These classic hits brought a group of siblings from Dania, Florida, into a sudden influx of fame and fortune. However, that would be short-lived as personal challenges began to cause discord, discontentment, and division within the group.

What is most intriguing is that you will hear the gospel message of Jesus Christ that has transformed Eddie's life. The title of this book is not just a creative cliché of a song he wrote, but it is more of a statement to encourage those who need to know that God is waiting on them. He is waiting for his lost and prodigal children to come back home to be greeted by His open arms.

I jumped at the chance to co-write this book with my dad for a couple of reasons. My first reason was to help him in any way possible, share his testimony with the world. Because in his testimony, he realized the necessity of turning back to God through repentance and following Jesus Christ.

By doing that, he was able to experience more profound joy, inner peace, and fulfillment in his life. It also guaranteed a place of permanent residency in heaven for his soul. I believe his story will bless many people because it is inspiring at best.

Secondly, it allowed me to find out fascinating things about my dad that I never knew. You see, I was not yet born when the group was establishing themselves in the music scene. I was a newborn baby when Too Late to Turn Back Now was on the US Billboard charts.

As you go through each page, I am sure that you will be able to identify with something mentioned in this book. This is how real and personal this book truly is.

Eddie was willing to be open and honest about sharing relevant information. He hopes that by opening up his life to the world, others going through similar situations will not satisfy the urge to give up on themselves.

Our prayer is that his testimony, helpful scriptures from the Word of God, and the substantial nuggets of wisdom through his experiences may encourage even one person to hold on and believe in the power of God's forgiving grace and love.

According to Eddie, "If God can change me, he can surely change anyone." Please enjoy the expressions of his heart put into words.

Teena Morena

INTRODUCTION

I t gives me great joy to tell my story to all of you. I give all the glory to God. I was not sure of how or when I would share my testimony, but the opportunity has presented itself at this time, and so I believe it's by God's will and grace that I share it with you now.

My story may have some familiar themes in it. After all, I was a music artist performing in the late '60s and 70s. During this time, many artists endured some of the same trials and troubles that I experienced personally. Yet, I do believe my story is unique as tailored to the calling that God has specifically for my life.

I want to give thanks to all my children, grandchildren, and great-grandchildren. I hope to leave you a legacy that will make you proud and give you a reason to smile. You are all my pride and joy. I love you, sincerely.

Thanks to Carter, Rose, and Billie Jo for being a part of a big dream that came true for all of us. Thanks to all of my siblings, family, and friends who have supported me throughout these years. I cannot name all of you, but you know who you are, and I hope you know my love for you is real.

A special thanks to my wife, Imer Cornelius. You continue to demonstrate an unconditional love that has stood through the test of time.

You are indeed an amazing woman, and I am glad that God has joined us together.

This book is not merely about the life and times of the Cornelius Brothers and Sister Rose singing group, but rather a book that gives an account of my testimony. The intention is to encourage that one lost soul or backslider to come back to their heavenly Father through Jesus Christ. I hope to honor God with my story and share with you the gift of knowledge that my life experiences have taught me.

I will share how God brought me through many of life's difficulties. I know that with each day I am given, I can do something more to bring glory to God, my Creator. If you are reading this book right now and you feel like giving up because you have gone too far off track STOP! Think again! It's NOT too late to turn back NOW!

CHAPTER 1

PREDESTINED

Me at 3 months old

Back To The Beginning

I guess it would be appropriate to give you the essentials before we get right into the heart of my story. Therefore, I will start with the basic details of my life.

I was born on June 19, 1943, to Florene Cornelius and Eddie Lee Cornelius Sr.

My parents met while my dad was in the army. He was stationed in Oklahoma where he met my mother. My mother was an educated woman who loved music and teaching. My dad also loved music and was a part of a gospel singing group in the military. My mother was quite charmed by my dad. They courted each other for a short while, fell in love, and then got married.

A few years after starting a family, my parents moved from Oklahoma to Miami, Florida. We stayed there for a short while but moved once again to Dania Beach, Florida., which became our permanent residence.

My dad was a licensed master plumber who owned his own plumbing business. My mother was the business manager of their plumbing company and a homemaker.

I remember my dad worked long hours every day completing service calls while my mother worked from home and took care of all the kids. I was the oldest of the 10 kids they had together. It was quite common to have big sized families back in those days, so having ten or more kids would not have earned you your reality TV show. I did not know it back then as a child, but as I grew up, I realized that my mom had the hardest job.

Aside from helping run the business, my mom would also cook meals throughout the day (no fast food), help with the farming and keeping of the animals, do the house cleaning, oversee the children, clean all the pots and dishes (no dishwasher), sew, wash the laundry (no washer and dryer) help with budgeting and sorting of all the bills. For our large family, it was like running a small company. However, most of the time, momma made it look super easy.

I can remember my mom having such a kind heart. She was indeed a genuine and loving person. Now don't get me wrong, she would spank our behinds when we got out of line, but afterward, she would do something sweet to show us that it was out of love and concern for us.

Like most children, we did things that would disappoint our parents. I was the child that was always busy with my hands. I loved fixing and rigging up different things that I could find around the house. The problem was that sometimes I would fix things that didn't need repair. I would typically find out the hard way that if it ain't broke, don't fix it.

I remember going through and breaking some of my sisters' baby dolls just so that I could fix them up the way I thought they should work. I would take out the recorders inside the talking dolls to figure out their mechanism.

I credit my dad for these skills. He was so mechanically inclined, and I admired that about him. He taught me a lot about plumbing, carpentry, and working with my hands. Although my dad could fix and build just about anything, plumbing was his main business, and I learned it as trade too.

Something else that I admired about him is the fact that he was the first black master plumber in our hometown. He was a hardworking man who studied his craft and took pride in his work. Learning these traits from my dad has been essential to my success. It made it possible for me to earn a living doing something that I truly enjoyed.

The Hosting Family

Just like any other family, we faced several challenges. We learned different ways to help deal with things. One way was to occupy our time with fun and entertainment. We had friends over a lot. There were not many dull moments in our home. I felt our family had a magnetic charm about us, especially since we drew many of the neighborhood kids to our house. On the other hand, maybe it was because we were one of the first families in our neighborhood who owned a TV. Hmmm….

My mom would always welcome our playmates and friends. As I said, she had a kind and generous heart towards everyone. If my momma didn't like you, there was something wrong with you.

We did some small farming too, and we kept animals growing up. I mean, we had cows, bulls, and all sorts of other farm animals around. We would milk the cows (which I hated to do) early in the morning. I remember my brother John got up first to milk the cow right before we had to go to school. That is pretty much what you had to do if you wanted milk for breakfast.

The bulls were quite exciting for me because they were so big and strong. I knew it was dangerous and crazy to ride those bulls, but I thought it was the most exciting thing to do back in the day. I would say the thrill of it might be like the thrill of bungee jumping or sky diving for today's generation.

As natural entertainers, my siblings and I would have a little rodeo show in the yard on the weekends. It drew a small group of onlookers in the neighborhood sometimes. Even at an early age, it intrigued me to perform in front of people. Bull riding was great entertainment, even if our parents did not think so. It was all in having a little fun, I guess.

Family Ties

Rodeo days

We did what all healthy kids did in our neighborhood during that time. We played together, picked on each other, took care of each other, and oh yeah, we fought each other too. Unfortunately, we were not always as close as a family. There were times when we did not get along. I still believe that we loved one another; we didn't always know how to show it.

In most of the large families that grew up in our neighborhood, at least two siblings usually bonded well together. I would have to say that my brother Carter and I fit that description. We were two peas in a pod. Carter and I would hang out even though I was five years older than he was.

He was the typical little brother looking up to his older brother, and he always wanted to tag along with me. At times, I would try to leave Carter behind to hang out with my friends that were my age. That didn't go over to well as he would start crying and carrying on so much. I would finally give in and tell him to come on. He wanted to come with me everywhere I went. Who would have ever thought that the two of us would eventually end up being the start of a successful singing group? God works in mysterious ways.

I would love to tell you more stories about all the different things I did with all my brothers and sisters. Unfortunately, that would take up the entire book. For the most part, we were your typical African- American family growing up during the late '40s, '50s, and '60s.

Raised In The Church

I make no joke about it; We were raised in the church. I had been in church all my childhood life, but I did not make that perfect connection with the Lord until many years later.

I can remember watching television on Easter Sundays. The TV stations would show programs on the crucifixion of Jesus Christ all day. I would sit there, watch it, and then cry. It drove me to tears every time I saw Jesus suffering like that. It moved me in the deepest part of my soul.

In the church we attended, I was a Jr. Deacon and then I moved up to work with the Sunday school. My mother would give us a dime (which was a big deal for us back then) so that we could put something in the offering plate.

Going to church as a kid felt normal, and I did it for a while. Unfortunately, I wandered away from the church when I reached adulthood. I became more interested in doing the things that I should not have been doing if you know what I mean.

Mama, I'm Grown!

I never doubted that God had a calling on my life. I accepted the Lord as my Savior, but I was not quite ready to make Him Lord and Master of my life at that time. I wanted to control things in my own life experience, and when I turned 18, no one could make me do anything that I didn't want to do.

Mama did her part to get us where we needed to be as kids. She was a faithful Christian who taught us God's Word and gave us the foundation of our faith. As I became an adult, the desire to rebel grew stronger.

Eventually, I stopped going to church altogether. The world seemed to offer a more appealing package, which made it easier to forget about serving God and going to church.

My mother was disappointed by some of my decisions, but she knew that the scripture of Proverbs 22:6 held strong, "Train up a child in the way he should go that when he grows old, he will not depart from it." I thank God for my momma's obedience to Him and her constant prayers over my life. It has indeed paid off.

We all looked forward to going to church back then as kids. It meant getting dressed up in our Sunday best, meeting up with our friends, going to Sunday school, and then eating a good Sunday dinner afterward.

It was a good thing for us to experience, and my mom knew that. She couldn't keep us from doing stupid things, but she believed that by getting us rooted in God and the church, we had a much better chance of having an abundant life.

Journey Into Manhood

In 1961, I graduated from Attucks High School and attended a local junior college. During college, I decided to be all that I can be and join the Armed Forces. I served in the Air Force during Vietnam, and then shortly after serving in the military, I started training to be an accountant in a local accounting institution.

Still searching for the right career, I decided to try my hand in working as an electrician. I gained experience in this line of work during my time in the Air Force, and this led me to get a job with Western Electric in South Florida.

I was the first black electrical installer hired in that area. After working with the company for a few months, I began to make a reputable name for myself.

I had obtained one of the highest scores on their in-house exams, and according to the company, I managed to achieve a distinct accomplishment.

The supervisor was so impressed; he came down from the corporate office in Jacksonville to our location in South Florida. He wanted to have the local newspaper write up an article on me. I'm not sure why, but I'm guessing it was more than just my high score.

I was grateful for the recognition and the job itself. I mean, who would mind getting an accolade or two? The article was nice, and the job was interesting enough to keep me going. However, music was a huge part of my core being.

EDDIE L. CORNELIUS WITH TEENA MORENA

CHAPTER 2
RISE TO STARDOM

Born To Sing

At the age of five, I started singing in local theaters and impersonating music moguls such as Nat King Cole, Louis Armstrong, and Roy Hamilton. I had a manly voice for a youngster, so it came quite natural for me to imitate adult male singers. At that age, I sang for fun, but that changed as I grew older.

At the age of 23, I wrote my first song, So Glad to Be Loved by You. This would be the beginning of a long list of songs. It was also during this time that I wrote Treat Her Like a Lady.

Writing songs became a common trend for me during this time. I began to slowly make my transition into the music business by looking for work as a songwriter. I figured I would get my foot in the door through songwriting and eventually become a recording artist.

I thought about creating lyrics for love songs and dance tunes as though it was a natural part of my day. For me, it was as common as getting up, eating breakfast, and brushing my teeth. I knew that I was determined to make music my profession. I just had to prepare and wait for the right opportunity to come my way.

It was not until I was much older when I understood the meaning of how God created us each with a unique purpose. Our gifts, talents, and leanings are in place before the first day of our actual physical existence.

Unfortunately, many times, circumstances in life pull us away from doing the things we were born to do.

I had my dreams and desires to make it into the music business, but I also knew I had to work and provide for my family until that happened. I was fortunate to have a great job while I still worked towards getting my dream job.

I remember thinking to myself that I can't get too comfortable with this 9 to 5 lifestyle. I didn't want to have a decent job stop me from doing something I loved more.

My Creator put the urge in my heart to write and sing songs. God knew me before I was in the womb of my mother. He knew He would save me; He also knew that I would be like the prodigal son and wander off.

He knew that I would fall into various temptations and lose it all. He knew that I would attempt suicide to end my life prematurely. He knew I would come back to Him and that He would be there waiting with open arms when I returned. That is still so awesome to me! From the very beginning, God knew what I would do, and He made it all work together for my good. Praise the Lord!

The Start Of Something Big

The Cornelius Brothers

As I mentioned earlier, God always has a perfect plan. Part of that plan was to pair me up with my younger brother Carter.

I had started singing around town at different clubs and juke joints in the area. During that time, my brother Carter (just like he did as a kid) decided to come along with me, and we both sang at these music spots.

One evening, while getting ready to go on stage at a local club, another band played a 15-minute set before us. It was an all-white teenage band, and they were pretty good. The group hung around after they played so they could hear us sing.

After we finished performing, a couple of the band members from that group came up to us. They said they were looking for lead singers for their band and asked if we would like to join them. Now keep in mind, this was not highly appreciated back in the late '60s. Segregation was still going strong in some places. However, we didn't care because we were all young, ambitious, and in love with good music.

My brother and I accepted the offer to be the lead singers for this new group. We called ourselves The Cape Crusaders.

Whenever we performed, Carter would have us put on these black capes as costumes. Although it may sound silly, we thought we looked cool. We made $15 a night singing in the local clubs.

After doing that stint for a little while, we decided to branch out on our own again. That is when we changed our name to The Cornelius Brothers. Things were beginning to change for the better shortly after that.

One day, my brother Carter told me about an ad in the paper from a producer seeking talented singers and songwriters. I was a little reluctant, but I did call the number listed to schedule an appointment.

On the day of our appointment, we drove down to this little office building in Miami, Florida. We met Mr. Robert Archibald, an executive producer that worked with Criteria Records.

I felt hopeful about this moment because I had been preparing for it for a while. Even though I was ready to get something going, I was still nervous. I didn't know if this producer would like us or if we were the type of talent he wanted for his project.

Once we walked into his office, we introduced ourselves and then took a seat in front of his desk. There was not a lot of small talks because he wanted to see other artists too. He had a "let's get straight to business" vibe about him, so that is what we did. I grabbed my guitar out of the case, and he said, "Okay, show me what you got!"

I started playing and singing songs from my list. I sang about five of my favorites, none of which seem to have impressed him. When I saw that he was not engaged it caused me to get discouraged. Archibald did not say one word, so after the fifth song, I decided we should leave and not waste any more of his time.

I told Archibald, "thanks for your time," and I took off my guitar strap to put the guitar back in its case. However, Carter didn't want me to give up. He stopped me and said, "Eddie, wait!" "Let him hear that song you wrote called Treat Her Like a Lady." I said to Carter, "If he didn't like those other songs, what makes you think he's going to like that one?"

Then Archibald said, "Well, let me hear it!" I took up my guitar again and started playing that song for him. Suddenly, I noticed he started moving his head and tapping his feet. Before I could even get to the next verse, he shouted, "Hey, wait a minute!" "I like that one!" "Let's record it!" I shouted back, "Man, are you serious?" Carter and I were screaming with joy. We were so excited to get this break. God was working it out. It seemed I saved the best song for last.

God used Carter to encourage me not to give up, and that night we signed our first record deal.

It didn't take long before Archibald started making preparations for us to go into the studio to record. Initially, we were scheduled to record at the Criteria Recording Studio in Miami, but Archibald decided to invest in a studio of his own.

While preparing to do our first recording, my mother thought it would be a good idea for us to include our sister Rose in our singing group. Carter and I talked it over and decided to follow through with momma's request. We asked Rose if she wanted to be a part of our group.

Rose agreed to join us, and we changed the name from The Cornelius Brothers to Cornelius Brothers and Sister Rose, and the rest is history.

Finally, we were on our way. It felt so good to get this opportunity. I had no idea what we were about to experience. All I knew was that it was indeed too late to turn back now. I continued writing songs as soon as they would come to my mind. It was as if I had some music-making factory going on inside of my brain. Speaking of music factory, that is what Archibald named his new studio. Our group was the first to record there.

When we went to our first recording session for Treat Her Like a Lady, I remember us going into the studio and having only four instruments on hand. We had the bass and electric guitar, drums, and a tambourine. That is what you hear now when you hear that song today.

When I wrote that song, I initially had Johnny Taylor in mind to sing it. I did not intend to sing it myself. That's why I didn't play it for Archibald initially. I had assumed that if I wanted to get my foot in the door, it would have to be as a songwriter first. Again, my plan was not exactly God's plan. Treat Her Like a Lady became a nationally known hit ranking number 3 on the Billboard Hot 100 and number 2 on the Cashbox top 100. In August of 1971, this song sold over a million copies which made it a certified gold record.

Celebrating our gold record with Bob Archibald

WE'RE OFF!

Immediately we started singing in many of the local spots in the South Florida area to promote our new record. It was getting great reviews all around. Local radio stations had started playing it in their rotation, and people were ordering boxes of these records to sell. By this time, we knew we were going up to a completely different level.

Archibald, our manager, had arranged for us to sign with United Artists for national distribution. Once Treat Her Like a Lady took off, we went from doing local gigs to doing large concerts. We were opening for notable artists in major cities across the country.

We were branching out into unfamiliar territory. We had never done large concerts, so this was all very new to us, but we loved it. It felt as though we were right where we belonged.

I will never forget our very first tour, which I believe started in Augusta, Georgia. We went there expecting to sing for just a handful of people, and it turned out to be a group of about 9,000 people.

In my mind, I thought that surely the crowd was there to see the other performing artists. However, when we came out to perform, we heard the crowd cheering so loudly that we could hardly hear ourselves singing. It was at that moment we discovered that we were no longer just three siblings from a small town trying to make it; we had officially made it.

People were asking for our autographs and for us to take pictures with them. It was indeed a new way of life for us. Now that we had a hit record on the charts, we were quickly making our way into the mainstream music scene.

We started singing at concerts with such famous people as Natalie Cole, Stevie Wonder, Al Green, James Brown, Brenda, and the Tabulations, The Ohio Players, Ike and Tina Turner, Leon Russell, Jean Chandler, Wilson Pickett, Jerry Butler and so many other great performers.

In my opinion, the '70s was a great time for African-American artists. We were finally getting better treatment in the places we booked.

One famous club, which was very hard to get into, was the Copacabana Club. We got booked there too! It was an excellent place for crossover artists or artists looking to become crossover artists. You knew you had arrived when you played at the Copacabana.

By this time, we were doing very well for ourselves. We had lots of gigs, good money coming in, and one gold record under our belt.

A Major Setback

While we were still on our first tour, we had arrived to perform in a small rural city in Texas. It was another sell-out performance. The audience was predominantly white, and I found that to be most intriguing. It felt good to know that our music was appealing to all different types of people.

It also felt great being on stage and seeing the audience responding so well to our performances. I decided to bring up on stage one of the women in the audience. I wanted to serenade her with one of the love songs. I was merely acting out as this was quite common for an artist to do in those days.

Well, by the look on her boyfriend's face, I could see that he did not take it that way. That was a minor thing though.

The next day, everyone in the band was in good spirits. We were feeling confident and proud of another successful show. We were most happy that we did not encounter any racial tension or altercations during the concert in that town. Unfortunately, the good feelings we had would not last long.

After packing everything up, the band got on the bus and headed out to the next city on the tour. I decided to drive my car and just follow the group there. Before leaving, my friend Stoney said: "Hey Eddie, I'll ride with you!" He jumped in the back seat and we headed out.

Stoney was a dear friend and he played guitar in the band. We were good buddies and we liked hanging out together. He was very protective and always had my back.

As we were driving to the next city on the tour, I noticed flashing lights behind me. It was a police officer pulling me over. I didn't understand why we were getting stopped, but of course, I did pull over to the side of the road.

The officer got out of the car and came to my window to talk to me. He said "Hi sir, I didn't mean to alarm you, but I went to your show last night and noticed you leaving the rest stop. I just wanted to ask if you would sign my copy of your Treat her like a lady record."

I was so relieved! I gladly got out of the car and leaned on my door while he went to get the record and pen out of his car. We talked for a couple of minutes, you know, just shooting the breeze.

During this time, Stoney had opened his door and stuck his head out to hear my conversation with the officer. Just as the trooper walked away, I looked up and noticed a truck swerving off the road and coming straight towards me.

It was coming at such a high speed; I didn't have time to do anything. I tried to protect myself by sticking my arms out like I was making a football block. That block was no match at all for that truck. Both Stoney and I got hit head-on. Stoney was hit first and he took a direct blow to his head. He was just getting out of the car and didn't see the truck coming.

I was standing when the truck hit, so the impact took me up in the air about 30 feet from the ground. I landed back on the hood and rolled onto the highway.

Cars were honking and swerving trying not to hit me, but I kept going in and out of consciousness.

I said, "Did he just hit me?" I looked down at my legs and noticed how they had turned backward like a pretzel. My body was unrecognizable to me.

Fortunately, none of my vital organs suffered any damage. I was in extreme shock! I did not feel any pain at first, but I was majorly shaken up.

As terrifying and devastating as this was, the most gripping experience of this whole event is still baffling me today.

As I was lying there on the ground, a strange man in a black suit stood over me. I could hardly see his face, but I'll never forget the voice. He had a strange, soft voice. He leaned in and then whispered over me "Do you believe in God?" And I answered, "Yes, I do!"

All I could see in the background around me was this unusual shade of green color. I mean, the whole area. Including the cars, the road, and everything around me were blocked behind this unique shade of green — a color like I had never seen before in my life.

However, the man who had asked me if I believed in God, was in his natural color. Once I told him, "Yes, I believe in God!" He replied, "That's all I wanted to know."

Immediately after that, he was gone and everything had turned back to its normal color. I know this may sound strange to some of you reading this, but this was not a figment of my imagination.

This man was not a paramedic, police officer, or anyone from the band and tour group. His question and his sudden disappearance made me believe that this man was some type of supernatural being.

The paramedics arrived shortly after that and started caring for me and Stoney. While the paramedics worked on me, I kept trying to lift my head to look over at Stoney. I wanted to see how he was doing.

While they were working on me, I remember hearing one of the paramedics yelling "Ooh boy, they're going to have to amputate this leg!" That was not what I wanted to hear at all.

The paramedics rushed us both to the local hospital. As they put us in our separate trauma bays, I could see them working on Stoney directly across from me in the emergency room.

They were trying to put a breathing tube in him because he was not responding appropriately. His injuries proved to be fatal, and it was nothing they could do to save his life. I watched my good friend die that night from a traumatic head injury.

I think my heart was too broken to focus on my physical pain. As the doctors were moving my body, they were wondering why I wasn't screaming in agony.

One of the doctors said, "What are you, some kind of Superman?" Of course, they did sedate me, and I was given strong pain medication to help. They took me into surgery that same night.

I suffered multiple fractures and injuries throughout my entire body. I experienced a concussion, severely crushed and broken right arm, left leg, and right foot. Thankfully they ended up not having to amputate my leg. The doctor consulted an animal surgeon who worked with horses. He was able to help with rodding and screwing my leg back into place.

My mind was going a mile a minute. I was grieving over Stony's death plus worried about having to cancel the tour and disappoint everyone. I also thought about my family, the group, and our manager. This was simply not a good time.

I couldn't help but wonder and ask God a lot of why questions. For instance, why did Stoney have to die? Why did God spare me from death? The other question that kept coming to my mind was; who was that man asking me if I believed in God?" I know that it was nothing short of a miracle for me to survive such a harrowing experience like that.

Once word got out that I was in the hospital, it aired on the local news. The report was that one of the Cornelius Brothers had been in a severe accident. What was so amusing was that since our song was such a cross over hit, some people did not know if we were African- American or white. Some of our fans were coming to the hospital looking for a white male. When they discovered that I was black, they could not believe their eyes.

You see, at that time, we did not have many of our pictures in publication all over the place yet. It is very different from today, where photographs and news post instantly on the internet. Even though people heard the song on the radio, not too many had seen our promo pictures yet. Some fans were confused about our identity in certain parts of the country, especially in Texas.

The Adding Of Another Sibling & The Making Of Another Hit Song

Cornelius Brothers and Sister Rose featuring Billie Jo

Immediately after the accident, our manager postponed the tour temporarily. Even though I was in the hospital for weeks, we had a hit record playing everywhere and we were booked in several venues. We were also under contract to have three singers at all our scheduled shows.

When I was released from the hospital and back at home in Florida, I decided to ask my sister Billie Jo if she would step in and do a few shows in my place.

The plan was for Billie to fill in for me and sing with the group until I completely recovered. We all came to appreciate the addition, so ultimately, we decided to have Billie continue as a permanent group member.

My focus during my recovery period was to hurry up, get back on the road, and start recording new music at the end of the tour. That was the same focus for my manager Archibald too.

During my in-home recovery, another popular group had contacted Archibald. It was Mr. and Mrs. Ike and Tina Turner. Once you start writing hit songs, other artists may inquire of you to write music for them as well. As a singer-songwriter, I was not only gaining recognition for singing, but I also gained recognition as being a songwriter.

As I mentioned earlier, songwriting was my original plan for breaking into the music business. I wanted very much to include writing music for others in my music career plans. It merely needed to be in the right space at the right time. My manager did not understand this.

It was not even a good week after my release from the hospital when Archibald called me with a proposition. He tells me that Ike and Tina Turner need a new song for their album and that he needed me to come down to the studio right away to meet with them.

I do not know what they discussed or what deal he was trying to work out with them. Archibald had a habit of making decisions for us on his own without giving us all the details of what was going on until later.

They had flown into town and wanted to offer me payment for some new material. I had no idea about the meeting, and this caused me to get very upset with my manager. He did not consider the fact that I was in the process of recovering and recently discharged from the hospital. So I told Archibald, "NO, I can't make your meeting today!"

Now I know you're probably saying to yourself," ARE YOU CRAZY!" Okay, now that I think about it, yes, I must have been a little bit crazy. Maybe it was a reaction from the pain medicine. Regardless, at that time, I was trying to prove a point. I also did not want to meet them in my condition.

My manager begged and pleaded with me to come down to his office to meet with them, but I flat out refused. Of course, he was livid with me, and I am sure that Ike and Tina were extremely disappointed too. They did not stay together much longer after that anyway, so I guess it was okay after all.

Shortly after that, my manager/ producer called me on the phone and said, "Look, Eddie! We are going to need a follow-up hit song for the next album. I need you to write something quick so we can record it!" I told him that I would get to working on something very soon.

I didn't come up with any new ideas for a new song right away. Typically when I write music, it comes naturally to me. In this case, I was under a lot of pressure to write a good song in a short matter of time.

On one particular day, I found myself getting frustrated and tired of trying to come up with the perfect song. I decided to go to bed early and get some sleep so I could relax and feel better.

While lying in my bed, I heard guitar strings strumming a new melody in my mind. Even though I was not touching my guitar, I could hear the strings clearly as if I were.

I tossed and turned a little, not really wanting to get out of bed, but then the melody wouldn't go away. I finally decided to get up and write the lyrics to the tune. The moment I got out my pen and paper, the words start flowing from my heart.

I knew what I wanted to say in this song—the words matched perfectly with the angelic melody. After completing the song, I laid back in bed and fell asleep.

The very next day, I called Archibald and let him know that I had written our next big hit song. That song was Too Late To Turn Back Now. I was confident about this song being a hit because of the way it came to me. I shared it with the group, and we got together to practice the song. I knew how I wanted the instruments and background vocals to sound on this record.

We released the song in 1972, and it would indeed become a hit record being certified gold, reaching number one on the Cash Box Top 100 and number two on the US Billboard charts.

Too Late To Turn Back Now and Treat Her Like a Lady are still two of the most sought-after songs of the '70s. These songs were a blessing sent from God. I knew he gave me the gift to write songs; however, I did not know how He would open doors for me with that gift.

I recently looked on the internet and saw a write up that said "Eddie has a melodic style of writing, and his lyrics have a way of staying with you." I pray that this is indeed true because now I am singing songs based on the Word of God. I hope that my songs of praise and adoration to God will stay on the heart of the listeners too.

Praise the Lord for providing me with the gift of songwriting and singing. Now I am writing songs to bring Glory to Him. Hallelujah to the Lamb of God!

TBH (The Big Head) Syndrome

Celebrity and wealth can tend to change a person in the worst ways. You can develop what I like to call TBH "The Big Head Syndrome" or an oversized ego.

It reminds me of the scripture in Matthew 19:23-24 "How hard is it for a rich man to enter into the kingdom of God?" "It's like squeezing a camel through the eye of a needle." Ouch! The words Jesus spoke did not have a lot of clarity to me at first, but I have an interpretation of what this verse could mean.

It is not that God does not want his children to have beautiful things and be well off. It is just that the love and worship of money cause us to lose sight of the more essential things in life, including our relationship with God.

Matthew 6:24 NIV reads this "No one can serve two masters. Either you will hate the one and love the other, or you will be devoted to the one and despise the other. You cannot serve both God and money."

Money equates to power, and if you aren't careful, too much of either can swell up your ego with arrogance and pride. You could quickly start thinking crazy ideas like "I alone am the reason for my success.", "No one else is as good as me" or "I don't need anyone telling me what to do..." Foolish pride unchecked can also create two other self-destructive offsprings: selfishness and greed.

I can see why it would make it hard for a rich person (who is serving their money) to do the will of God. Money should serve our needs, but we should never let money master over us. If money becomes an idol or a god in your life, you will never have enough to be satisfied. The more you have, the more you crave.

When you add fame to the mix, you have just changed the game completely. Fake friends will feed your ego by telling you everything you want to hear, pretending they care about you to get closer to your money. They will also use their association with you to gain influence and create opportunities for themselves.

For the fellas reading this, women who would not give you the time of day when you were just ordinary, will start throwing themselves on you without any shame.

They have no restraint or regard for your relationship status. These types only care about one status, and that is the financial one. I believe the commonly used term for this type of woman is "gold digger."

Opportunities will open up for you to buy lavish things you once could only afford in your dreams. Everyone from everywhere will start offering you the whole world in a handbasket, and some of these things being illegal if you know what I mean.

Here is the drawback, the moment you lose that money, and your popularity starts to fade is the moment you see everything, and every so-called friend, dissolve like ashes left over from a campfire.

What tends to happen often is that the lifestyle of the rich and famous is all too good to give up, and the fear of losing fame and money causes some people to become corrupt in their practices. Some even forsaking any moral obligation to those who are looking up to them as mentors or role models.

Now compare a big ego to a hump on a camel's back. The hole of a sewing needle is tiny and narrow. Nothing of enormous size as a camel's hump will go through it.

Now consider the kingdom of God. Anyone wishing to obtain entry into God's domain must first choose to seek God and His will first. If you are serving yourself or your money before God, you decide to live by your own rules, which means you also live by your own decisions, and you will deal with the consequences of those decisions.

If taking the red pill meant following Christ and the green pill meant doing things my way, I foolishly chose the green pill.

At the time, the illusion of being in complete control felt better than the actual truth. Reality came in like a wrecking ball knocking all of my imagined simulations down to the ground.

I would advise strongly, with as much strength as you can muster up, avoid getting TBH syndrome. Remain humble and stay grounded. Keep wise people around who will tell you the truth, even if you don't want to hear it. Keep family and friends who genuinely love you at close hand because they love you for who you are.

God gives grace to the humble but rejects the proud. If only I had known that back then. I believe I would have avoided so many of the pitfalls I encountered in my life.

I did not prepare for what was happening. At one moment, it felt like things were not moving fast enough. Once my music career took off, it felt as though things were moving too fast. I had to learn the pros and cons of sudden stardom very quickly.

Greener Grass Still Has Its Weeds

Although fame can be appealing, it can also be quite complicated. However, I think I figured it out. Here is my breakdown. Stardom brings you a lot of popularity, but it takes away your privacy. Stardom can bring you a lot of wealth, but it also makes you an easy target for pride, theft, and phony relationships.

You don't know who loves you for you anymore. Everybody is out to make a buck off you. Lawyers, agents, companies, etc.... You begin to center your life on trying to stay relevant. Eventually, when the party train comes to an end, most people find themselves getting off where they started, with nothing.

Our sudden success was causing increasing problems within our group. We would have intense arguments between the four of us. The most hurtful part was that we were siblings. I mean, this was my blood.

It seemed we allowed our selfish desires to consume our thoughts and lead us into bitter fights with each other. Now I know blood is thicker than water, but stubborn pride can make you forget all about that sometimes.

The enemy of our soul loves to cause strife and division. He loves to tear down families, churches, businesses, even nations.

Family is a primary target, and I believe it is because family is the foundation of our society. When families are healthy, focused, and united, it can be a mighty force against destroying Satan's kingdom.

Some of the best sports teams to ever win a championship did so because they worked together in unity. Unfortunately, we allowed our instant success to drive a big wedge between us, and our rise to sudden fame was about to fall hard and fast.

CHAPTER 3

THE PRODIGAL SON

Temptations

The year was 1973. We now had two top hits under our belt, and money was coming in on a good and steady flow. I bought cars, expensive clothes, jewelry, and anything else I wanted to buy. I also continued to cultivate my bad habits.

As I mentioned earlier, when you reach a certain status of fame, anything and everything goes. It was like a package deal. You get the recognition, but you also get a boatload of temptations and bad influences.

Everything that was initially hard to obtain became instantly available and accessible. Things like drugs, alcohol, women, gambling, and even satanic worship came tossed on a plate and thrown in my face like a roasted pig with an apple in its mouth.

Before my involvement in the entertainment business, I did not drink, or touch any drugs. After an overwhelming exposure to it all, I finally gave in to the pressure. The temptation to try new things became impossible to avoid while traveling on the road.

First, I started with drinking a beer on occasion. Then I gradually went from having one beer a day to drinking a fifth of liquor in about two days. I eventually tried cocaine (commonly used around our circle of musicians back then) and other drugs too.

I remember one incident that went very wrong during my experimenting phase. We were staying at a beautiful hotel that hired our group to perform. Before the show, one of the band members had given me a joint that had angel dust in it. I had never experienced angel dust, nor did I want to, but I figured it must be okay since my band member recommended it. BOY WAS I WRONG! When I smoked it, I went ballistic; I mean embarrassingly crazy. I was so out of control. It cost us that gig at the hotel and left me messed up for over a week. I pretty much stuck to drinking alcohol after that.

Satanic Sabotage

I know it's easy to blame the devil, and it's justifiable when you understand the war that is going on for your soul. I am convinced that SOME of the difficulties in our lives are not only by our own bad choices but also by what I call "satanic sabotage."

The enemy of God has been sabotaging God's children since the beginning of time. For example, the fall of Adam and Eve, found in the book of Genesis of the Bible, describes how Satan plotted and tempted Adam and Eve to sin against God.

Of course, it was ultimately their choice to disobey God that caused them to be cursed and banned from the Garden of Eden; however, there was no denying that the devil's contribution was a strong influence in this major downfall of humankind.

Because God loves us so much and wants us to live abundantly in our purpose, the devil works very hard to destroy you before you even have a chance to know your real meaning and calling in life.

The number one goal of the thief is to steal, kill, and destroy. One of the most significant attacks used by the enemy on a child of God is spiritual identity theft. If you do not know who you are, you could easily choose to live an altered life that is far from your created purpose and calling.

In the world system, especially in the entertainment world, many demons are calling you to live a hedonistic lifestyle. For a season, it feels good, but there are always repercussions.

I'm not just talking about something minor like a hangover. No! I am talking about a deeper burden of pain and sorrow that takes you to a place of major regret and depression.

I knew the struggle was a spiritual one. I had God on one side trying to pull me out of the darkness and the devil trying to force me to stay in it.

It's a constant battle we face every day between our spirit man and the natural man. The sinful lifestyle offered to me seemed so fun and appealing, but I didn't know the fun of that lifestyle would only last for a season. The consequences would soon begin to follow behind, and they were not worth the temporary satisfaction I enjoyed.

After a show, I would usually go back to my hotel room to sulk. I would feel utterly depressed and would sit there looking at the four walls. I sometimes cried out to the Lord to pray and ask Him, "How did I get like this?" "Because I'm not satisfied, I'm not happy with my life like this."

I would even pray aloud and tell the Lord, "I love you!" I would say that repeatedly while being drunk sometimes. I would be stumbling over myself, just saying, "Lord, I love you." It's too bad I wasn't drunk in the spirit.

I know now that it was the Holy Spirit prompting me to come back and fall in love with God the Father through Jesus. When you fall in love with someone or something, automatically, there is a drawing towards that person or thing.

God would continuously remind me that He had a calling on my life, but like the prodigal, I wanted to do things my way. I wanted to be in control even if it was only an illusion.

The Wander Years

I wandered around in the darkness for years. I had seen my life take a downward spiral spiritually and physically. I got so far from the Lord that I started making more of the wrong decisions for my life. I was partying, using drugs, sleeping with other women, drinking alcohol, and overspending money.

Violence and depression were becoming more and more of a regular pattern for me. No matter how I tried, I could not break the cycle. It was slowly destroying me, and I had no control over it.

I knew I didn't want to live that way, but I couldn't bring myself to giving it up completely. Satan had a stronghold on my life, and I allowed it for a long time.

During this time, our group was still traveling and selling records. I continued to write and record more songs like I'm Not Your Big Time Lover, Never Gonna Be Alone Anymore, and Let Me Down Easy. Our shows continued to do well. So naturally, I was in no rush to change my lifestyle. I was enjoying my celebrity status to the point that not only had I wandered away from God, but I also wandered away from my family at home.

Love and Marriage

I met my first wife in college before we formed the singing group. We were both young and ambitious with a lot of dreams to accomplish. Like many young couples, we felt that we could easily live out our lives happily ever after.

In the early part of our marriage, things seem to be quite normal. However, when my music career started taking off, things started to drastically change, and it wasn't for the better.

It would be easy to say that many of the problems in my first marriage came by way of my music career, but that would be an unfair statement. The increasing attention and notoriety may have played a small part, but it was much more than that causing issues.

I didn't have the right attitude to be a good husband at that time. It was all about me during those years. Everything had to be done my way. I was young, proud, and foolish. I couldn't see that back then.

One of the most amazing things I had ever experienced in my life was becoming a father for the very first time. It amazed me to see the miracle of childbirth. I thought, "How could God trust us to care for something so tiny and precious?" At that moment, I thought, "Surely this is what I needed to get my focus where it should be. I was feeling good and loving my role as a new father. We had three children together and for a while, it renewed my hope that my marriage and our family would be okay.

As beautiful as it was being a husband and a dad, I was also thrilled to be singing and performing on stage. My schedule grew even more hectic, and my time with my family had become less and less. I started to develop a separate life on the road, and I was getting myself involved in all types of bad situations. The double lifestyle I was living became challenging to maintain, but by then, I had developed deeply buried roots of sin that I did not want to pull up.

One major temptation for me was the lure of women. Living one way on the road and another at home was creating so much confusion. I couldn't keep the two lifestyles separate anymore. Instead of stopping the bad behaviors that I practiced on the road, I started to behave like another person at home.

I was mistreating my wife and looking for opportunities to be with other women. Before I knew it, I had formed committed relationships that led to having children outside of our marriage.

As I continued my life outside of God's will, my first wife finally had enough and wanted out. She could not put up with my destructive lifestyle anymore.

I hated what I was doing to her, but I didn't know how to change my behavior. The truth of the matter is that I didn't want to change at that time. As I said earlier, I wanted to do things my way, and I wanted her and everyone else to accept that. She didn't, and our marriage ended.

After my first wife and I divorced, I found myself getting more involved with another woman named Imer. She had two daughters from a previous marriage that I raised as my own and we started having children together. Although we were building a family, I was not ready to change from my womanizing ways.

I was still struggling to find love and happiness, and I was looking for love in all the wrong places. I needed God's love. Instead, I continued to act as though I didn't need Him or His love. I continued hurting myself and others because hurt people, hurt people.

On top of everything being spiritually and morally wrong in my life, I was also dealing with the deadly combination of anger, depression, stress, alcohol, drugs, and fatigue. I was a ticking time bomb just waiting to explode, and eventually, that is what I did.

I started arguing with Imer over everything simply because I was miserable. I would get so angry that I would start yelling and throwing things all around the house.

On stage, I was different. I can remember seeing the fans screaming and shouting while I sang those love songs. It was easy to look and sound convincing to a bunch of strangers who didn't know me. That was part of my act.

Once I got off the stage, things were very different. When the lights and cameras were gone, so was my ability to hide from my pain.

I had pressure coming from every direction, and I didn't know how to handle it. I could hardly meet the demands of our manager, the booking agents, my parents, my siblings, and the mothers of my children.

The more I wandered away from who God created me to be, the more I didn't like myself. The enemy had me bound in these chains, and the strongholds were slowly breaking me down.

My personal life was in a complete shambles, but my music career was right where I wanted it to be. So at least I thought.

Fool's Gold

The devil knew how to make everything look so good and enticing, but we all know that looks can be deceiving.

The whole showbiz circle was like riding on a rollercoaster. One minute you're up, and the next minute you're down. Believe me, when you come down, you are coming down hard. When you think you've had enough, you find out that it's even harder trying to get off that ride. You get strapped in tight, and you can't get off so quickly.

Temptations are common to man; we all have been or will experience this in life. Thankfully, God gives us a way out of each one. It is up to us to make the right choices in life or deal with the consequences. I was making many of the wrong decisions in my life during this time.

I should have been dead. I should not even be alive to write this book and share this story of my life. Yet, I can testify that if it had not been for the Lord on my side, I would not be here. He has spared my life for such a time as this.

As my career soared, I wandered further and further away from the Lord. I had allowed so many different things to become idols, and the more I worshipped these idols, the more I put God on the back burner.

What was I thinking? That is just it! I was not thinking. I was not concerned about God, my life, my loved ones, or the consequences of my choices.

Oh, but God would not give up on me that easily. No matter how far I wandered away, He knew exactly where I was and how to get my attention when he needed to.

The Break-up

My hat goes off to the groups that have stuck together for many years — music groups like the Rolling Stones, Isley Brothers, and Earth Wind and Fire. I do have a respect for that type of loyalty and dedication because being in a group IS NOT EASY.

I loved being with my brother and sisters in our singing group. It was a blessing and an opportunity of a lifetime. It was a miracle to come from a small town like Dania, FL, and make global hit records.

I believe God had ordained us to achieve more than we had ever imagined. Yet because of tension, disagreements, and ongoing conflicts, our group failed to accomplish success to its fullest potential.

In 1976, 2 years after releasing our mild hit records, Don't Ever Be Lonely and I'm Never Going To Be Alone Anymore, the group broke apart.

We each decided to go in different directions in pursuing our music careers and other endeavors.

We weren't the first group to ever break up. It has happened to some of the biggest and best groups in show business. Maybe for some of the same reasons that our group did.

Regardless of the reasons, I can tell you firsthand that it was hurtful. After all, we were still family. It was hard dealing with the frustration of the group coming to an end. Especially knowing the negative impact it would bring on our family and fans.

I know we each had a calling on our lives before we were even born. Our mother had already planted the seeds when we were little, and the enemy wanted to destroy us before we could reach our true destinies.

Sadly, we allowed this failure to happen. Somehow, we managed to turn the blessing God had given us into a curse. I believe it was because God was no longer who we aimed to please first.

Now I know this is just my outtake on the matter, but I believe it was a huge part of why our group ended. I still love all of my family, and I regret many things that have happened in the past. If I knew what I know now, I would have done some things differently.

I was feeling lots of sadness, frustration, bitterness, and disappointment during this time. Daily I encountered dreadful thoughts of all my failures and constant fears of losing everything.

I remember being so depressed and discouraged, I thought the best thing to do was simply end my life. One night, while sitting on the bed in my hotel room, I took my gun out of my overnight bag. At first, I just stared at it. Tears started flowing down my face like a steady stream. I put the gun up against my forehead. I thought it would be the perfect escape to put an end to all my pain and anguish.

I gently touched the trigger on the gun and I closed my eyes real tight. In a quick second, I saw a vision of my kid's faces flash across my mind.

All of a sudden, I froze with fear! I threw the gun down on the floor. I was so close to making a horrible decision. It had to be an angel of God that stopped me from ending my life that night.

Listen, I sympathize with anyone who has considered or died from suicide. Depression is a severe illness. If not treated, it can lead to major problems, including premature death. God's grace kept me, and it is still what I rely on today.

Although the group had dismantled, we were still under a recording contract. Naturally, lawsuits from promoters, record executives, and even our manager/producer Archibald bombarded us almost immediately when the news came out of us breaking up.

There was no hope of us getting back together, so we each tried to make solo careers or start new bands using the same original group name.

We had two groups booking gigs with the name Cornelius Brothers and Sister Rose. This issue confused booking agents, so eventually, I stopped getting a lot of gigs.

CHAPTER 4

BROKENNESS

Pride Comes Before A Fall

Instead of using this as an opportunity to seek God, I did the complete opposite. I got so angry with God. I began doing things just to spite Him.

I convinced myself that I did not need to wait on God's timing anymore to have my best life. As usual, I was going to take matters into my own hands.

It reminds me of a story in the Bible concerning King Saul. He was king of the Israelites after they begged God to give them a king to rule and lead over them.

Initially, King Saul was humbled and very committed to the ways of God. However, over time, he became prideful and more concerned about how he could please himself and the people versus how he should please God.

It also became prevalent for King Saul to take matters into his own hands without waiting on God's timing and guidance. Ultimately, after multiple rebellious acts, God chose Saul out of his position as king of Israel.

One story of Saul's rebellious response to God depicts Saul preparing his men for war against the Philistines. Before they were to set out for battle, Saul wanted to know what would become of him and his sons as they faced the Philistines in battle.

His friend, the prophet Samuel, had already died. Samuel was the prophet God used to anoint Saul as king and to give Saul His counsel and instructions. After Samuel's death, Saul was no longer getting God's specific word or counsel. Yet, that did not stop Saul from trying to get his answers another way.

Saul decided to summon a medium or witch of En-dor. This action was evil, as God is against any sorcery, divination, or witchcraft.

Even Saul himself had ordered all witches banned from the land as a response to God's command and displeasure for this evil activity.

Since Saul was not sure of how to get God to speak to him concerning his fate, he took matters into his own hands. Here is the scripture below for reference.

1 Samuel 28: verses 7-19

7) *Then Saul said to his servants, "Seek for me a woman who is a medium that I may go to her and inquire of her." And his servants said to him, "Behold, there is a woman who is a medium at En-dor."* 8) *He disguised himself by putting on other clothes and went, he and two men with him and they came to the woman by night; and he said, "Conjure up for me, please, and bring up for me whom I shall name to you."* 9) *Then the woman said to him, "Look, you know what Saul has done, how he has cut off the mediums and the spiritualists from the land. Why then do you lay a snare for my life, to cause me to die?"* 10) *Saul vowed to her by the LORD, saying, "As the LORD lives, no punishment shall come upon you for this thing."* 11) *Then the woman said, "Whom shall I bring up for you?" And he said, "Bring up Samuel for me."* 12) *When the woman saw Samuel, she cried out with a loud voice; and the woman spoke to Saul, saying, "Why have you deceived me? For you are Saul. Why are you then laying a snare for my life to bring about my death?"... 13) The king said to her, "Do not be afraid, but what do you see?" And the woman said to Saul, "I see a divine being coming up out of the earth."* 14) *He said to her, "What is his form?" And she said, "An old man is coming up, and he is wrapped with a robe." And Saul knew that it was Samuel, and he bowed with his face to the ground and did homage.* 15) *Then Samuel said to Saul, "Why have you disturbed me by bringing me up?" And Saul answered, "I am greatly distressed; for the Philistines are waging war against me, and God has departed from me and no longer answers me, either through prophets or by dreams; therefore, I have called you, that you may make known to me what I should do."... 16) But*

Samuel replied, "Why ask me since the Lord has left you and has become your enemy? 17) The Lord has done just as he said he would. He has torn the kingdom from you and given it to your rival, David. 18) The Lord has done this to you today because you refused to carry out his fierce anger against the Amalekites. 19) What's more, the Lord will hand you and the army of Israel over to the Philistines tomorrow, and you and your sons will be here with me. The Lord will bring down the entire army of Israel in defeat."

Saul had made his fair share of bad decisions. As humans, this is what we do, and God is fully aware of that fact. However, Saul's heart was hardened with pride, and he showed no repentance for his evil actions. This caused God to take away his anointing and give it to someone else who truly had the humility and a heart for God.

Pride created a wall between Saul and the Lord. This pride would ultimately be the cause of his fall. Like King Saul, I was far away from God. I allowed sin to drive a wedge between us, and the relationship suffered for a while. Eventually, I had stopped hearing the voice of God too.

When I tell you that I was broke, I mean, I couldn't rub two pennies together kind of broke! Most of my royalties from the songs I had written were going towards fighting my former manager/producer Archibald in lawsuits.

I had to hire an attorney to research every detail of my music, contracts, financial transactions, etc. It didn't matter what information I presented; I still could not match up to my former manager and his lawyers in court. When all the dust cleared, it left me with hardly anything.

Initially, I had a hard time getting any bookings for shows because word had gotten out that the group had broken up.

Since I had not yet established a solo career or produced a solo album, it was hard promoting myself as a solo artist. I hired a few singers and formed another group, and that got me a few gigs here and there, but it was not enough to pay all the bills. I had no job and no prospects of getting a job.

Money was slowly coming in; I could barely afford to support us. So there I was with no money, no work, and no place to go. I thought for sure that I had to be the most unfortunate man in the world.

Imer and I would argue constantly and she would threaten to leave me. We kept this destructive cycle going on for years.

I couldn't believe that the same person who had sung before big crowds of people was now sitting at home without a clue of how or where to find a job that would help support the family.

It became a constant project of trying to avoid eviction from our home. I was also trying hard to keep food in the house. Money was so scarce we struggled to keep the utilities on most of the time.

The fall from fame came so quick and hard. One minute I was up and making big moves with my music career, and within a few short years, I was out of work and in over my head with debt.

Thankfully, I still had my plumbing and electrical skills. I knew I could work with my hands, so I looked for work as an electrician or plumber.

Since I had been singing on the road for a few years, I did not have a resume with current work experience. Naturally, with the significant gaps in employment, it did not make me a stand out candidate for most of the well-paying jobs.

To bring in some income, I became a self-employed maintenance man. I promoted myself through referrals and word of mouth. My dad worked for himself for years in his own plumbing business, and since he had a reputable name in the area, I was able to get a few jobs by association.

That would help bring in some money, but it wasn't a consistent source of income. Without having a steady financial flow, it would often leave our family on the brink of losing everything.

It was not easy for me to go out into public settings because I knew that folks in my hometown would recognize me and wonder why I was working as a plumber and not singing. I did what I had to do, but this was such a humbling time for me.

Imer worked as well and did her best to help contribute towards the bills. I also found another way to earn money by fixing bicycles for the neighborhood kids. I set up a small workshop in my backyard to fix broken bikes. Honestly, I repaired most of them for free or dirt-cheap because most of my customers were kids. I would still get a few calls from former booking agents to do a singing gig here and there, but it was not steady enough to make a decent living.

No matter how hard we tried to budget, with the small amount of money we had coming in, we were continually struggling. Like the prodigal son in the Bible, I felt like I was in the pigpen scrapping for anything I could get. I had gotten down to the lowest point of my life. I knew God did not choose this life for me; I did! It was all because of my unwillingness to trust Him with my life.

I thought that all I needed to do was figure out a way to get up out of my situation quick, fast, and in a hurry. I tried hiring a lawyer to reverse the hold on my songwriting royalties. Unfortunately, the lack of money, multiple lawsuits, and previously signed contracts were all working against me. I didn't have a fighting chance.

It felt like my pockets had holes in them. Any money I made was going out so fast towards bills, and I could hardly keep anything. I had either pawned or sold everything I had that was valuable.

After trying to swing it for as long as we could, we finally could not hold on to our home any longer. The eviction papers were processed, and we were on the streets and homeless.

We packed up all of what we could take with us. Imer and I took the kids and went out to find housing and food. We didn't have much, but with the little money we had left, we hit the motel strip on the main highway by the beach.

We would stay a couple of nights and then leave at the break of dawn before anyone could see us. We went from motel to motel until we finally ran out of money.

Finally, I had to break down and ask my mom if she would allow us to stay with her until I got back on my feet. All I felt I could do was wait for a big break. I remember wanting a significant sum of money to come from somewhere.

Just like all the millions of other wishful people out in the world, I tried my hand in gambling. I played the lottery and even started going to the horse track to see if I could get lucky. I held on to hope that I would hit it big with a huge win. That way, I could at least get a house and put a dent in our bills. That did not work out so great either. Most of the time, we would lose the little money we had started with.

During that time, I also continued to find maintenance work around town. That would give me just enough money to get food and keep gas in the car for the week, so I could go back out again to find more work.

No matter what I did, it seemed nothing was working quickly enough to get me out of the hole I was in. I lived in constant regret for so many of the bad choices I made. I did not know how I was going to correct these things. All I knew was that I was broken.

I thought money would be the answer to my problems. WRONG AGAIN! I would constantly think to myself, "If I just had enough money, my life would be better, and we would be fine. I would also say, "If I could just get a new record deal and back on the road again with my singing, all things would go back to normal."

Well, my idea of "normal" was not a good vision to pursue. None of these ideas I had were the right solutions for my life to improve. It took time for me to realize that the same temptations and demonic vices were still waiting on me to get back out on the road too.

Peace of mind became foreign to me. I had this rage in my heart that would not go away. The four strongmen of anger, guilt, frustration, and depression were my steady companions.

These negative emotions were always controlling my everyday actions.

The change I needed to make was a supernatural one. I needed to be born again! I needed to have the Holy Spirit consume me with His all-consuming fire.

Only God could save me from hell and self-destruction. I needed His peace, His joy, and all the fruits of God's spirit. I needed to have a transformation. So why didn't I do what I needed to do to get that?

It's like when some of us know in our minds that we should eat less junk food and exercise more to feel better, but we don't because that would mean we'd have to give up things we like.

I would say my situation was similar to that. I had the head knowledge, but not a willing heart. It was a heart issue at the root of my dysfunction. Thankfully, God is the King of hearts too!

Ezekiel 36:26 King James Version (KJV)

26 A new heart also will I give you, and a new spirit will I put within you: and I will take away the stony heart out of your flesh, and I will give you a heart of flesh.

Still Running

When I think of running away from God, I always think of one popular story of a prophet in the Bible. The prophet named Jonah. I could surely relate to this man, although my reason for running was not the same as Jonah's reason. I connect to the part of running away from doing God's will, as Jonah did in the Bible story.

In case you don't know the story, I will give you a summary as a backdrop. Jonah was a minor prophet sent by God to deliver a message to the people of Nineveh. It was a small town, but very well known for its vicious and heinous acts towards one another and to other people throughout the nearby cities.

Jonah didn't think too fondly of these people, and like many others, he wanted to see this city and all its citizens destroyed for their evil acts.

Because Jonah knew God's character, he knew how God would respond in mercy towards the Ninevites if they sincerely repented. Instead, Jonah opted to run in the opposite direction and not tell the people of Nineveh God's message of repentance. The message was simple and clear, either you repent or be destroyed.

Jonah decided that he would not deliver this message and got on a boat to get as far away from the city of Nineveh as he could. Consequently, he could not get away from God.

As the story goes, Jonah paid a fare to sail out onto the sea on a merchant ship. Shortly after the ship sailed off, a strong storm came abruptly upon the sea. The ship crew was skilled in handling these types of situations, so they immediately began to unload cargo to keep them from sinking.

However, Jonah knew that this was not an ordinary storm, but rather an act of God's judgment towards him. He told the crew to throw him overboard to save themselves. They did not agree initially, but when it became clear that this was the only way for survival, they conceded with Jonah's request and threw him overboard.

Waiting for him in the sea was a big fish that swallowed him up and stored him in its belly. Jonah would sit in the darkness for three days and three nights praying to the Lord in repentance. God listened, responded with mercy, and then commanded the fish to let him go. The fish hurled him out of his belly and back onto dry land.

God then told Jonah once again, "Go tell the Ninevites the message I gave you!" It took all of 3 days for Jonah to go throughout the city of Nineveh to give them the message of repentance from God. They heard, they repented, and God saved them.

If Jonah had done that in the first place, he would have saved himself some suffering those three days he spent inside the dark belly of the big fish.

I pass no judgment on Jonah because, as I said earlier, I can relate! Although I knew that I should have done some things differently and that God was not pleased with my choices, I was not about to give up my ways. I just kept running and running as far as I could from Him. The good news is this; He never lost sight of me. To whoever is reading this right now, He has not lost sight of you either.

I had my fair share of storms in my life and many moments of darkness and despair. It was much later that I came to my senses and sincerely repented. Just like Jonah, the people of Nineveh, and many others before me- I received another chance to receive God's mercy and forgiveness, and so can you!

My Hands Were Tied

Let me say that whether you are saved or unsaved, we all must deal with some difficult situations in our lives. The major difference for us who follow Christ is that our anchor and strength comes through our Lord Jesus Christ. We don't have to go through trouble times alone or without His peace.

When I wasn't following Christ, I endured some difficult things in my life without the peace and comfort that comes from knowing the Lord. My so-called solutions to numbing my pain did not help my recovery in the long term. In many ways, it delayed it and even caused more pain.

Because of my faith background in the church as a youth, I was not entirely without a knowledge of God's power.

Although I was doing many of the wrong things, I knew enough to call on Jesus to help me out sometimes. I credit my sanity to God's grace and mercy on me. I know I would have completely lost my mind, and my life was it not for His grace and mercy.

My hard times created a pressure on me that was steadily breaking me down. Long after the group had broken up, the tension was still thick between us. My relationships with my wife and kids were not in the best of shape either. I depended on all the wrong things to get me through the daily challenges of life.

In the early '80s, I decided to make a comeback with new music as a solo artist. I got a call from an old friend of mine who let me know about a producer in Nashville who was interested in working on producing a solo album with me. It was a huge change, but it seemed like just the change I needed for my life at the time.

I moved to Nashville on my own, and my family stayed in Florida in a home I rented from my brother. I planned to wrap up the album in 3 months and then move my family with me after that.

Once I moved to Nashville, I shared an apartment with a longtime friend of mine. He was also trying to get back into the music business as a singer. We put together a duo act, like the once-famous duo Sam and Dave.

I had contacted a booking agency in the area, and they were able to get us a recurrent stint at a couple of the music venues nearby. I was also recording music for my new solo album.

After I completed the 1st album called For You, I moved my wife and kids from Florida to Nashville. The album didn't do so well. The label decided to go in a different direction with my sound. We started working on the next album and it was titled My Hands Are Tied. It had a nice mixture of R&B, pop, and country soul. I loved every single song we produced. I believed in all my heart that this was the breakout opportunity to jump-start my career as a solo artist.

After the completion of the 2nd album, my anticipation grew increasingly. Months had gone by, and I did not hear anything from the record label about a release date. I decided to call the record company to find out when the album would be released. When I finally got some information on the delay, it was nothing but bad news.

Shortly after wrapping up production, the record label went bankrupt. All the work and time I spent was for nothing. It left me with nothing but unpaid bills and lost hope. We came back to Florida with no money and no prospects in sight. As hard as times had become, nothing compared to what happened next.

Around midnight on Jan 10, 1985, I got a terrible phone call. My mother called me to let me know that my dad had suffered a stroke. He died on that same night. Our family would have to come together and deal with one of the toughest ordeals in life.

My dad taught me everything I knew. I didn't expect him to leave us so soon, but he was called home to the Lord. I don't know what the saddest part was for me; losing my dad or seeing my mom so devastated by losing her husband of many years.

I can still remember the hurt and grief on her face. After two years of widowhood, my sweet mama Florine died from a heart attack. When mama died, I was inconsolable. Within just two short years, both of my parents were gone.

My parents: Mr. and Mrs. Eddie Lee Cornileus Sr.

God Kept Me

Imer and I were still together, but we were still having problems. During our relationship, I had fathered more children from other women. I was now a father of 14 kids. As you can imagine, the financial and emotional stress did not make things any easier for our relationship.

As I mentioned earlier, I attempted to kill myself to stop my pain, but that was not the only time I considered it. I contemplated killing myself on multiple occasions. I collected guns and knives mostly for protection and for collection. The temptation to use them on me was dominant at this point in my life.

It was so hard for me to get any peace of mind. I lived in constant torment that even when things would get a little better, happiness would only last for a short period.

My children were starting to act out of their frustrations too. As they became teenagers, they started noticing things a lot more. They could see that things were out of order. The on and off arguing, along with the money struggles, were a regular part of our everyday life. They would get angry and frustrated about how we were living.

I did the best I could to help take care of my kids. Still, nothing would prepare me for what happened next.

I got a phone call from the mother of my youngest child. And this was the kind of call no parent ever wants to get. She called me to tell me that my youngest son had died in his sleep. He was only a few months old.

The medical examiner said that his death was from natural causes. I tried hard to understand what was going on, but I really couldn't wrap my brain around it.

I felt helpless and full of grief. I was not there the day it happened, and I could do absolutely nothing to console his mother. We were both grief-stricken and needed help from God to give us peace, strength, and comfort to get us through the pain.

Don't Ever Be Lonely (by Eddie Cornelius)

Don't ever be lonely (a poor little fool like me)

Don't ever be lonely, a poor little fool like me.

Don't ever be lonely, a poor little fool like me.

Oh, I sit down, and I moan sometimes.

Over a big mistake, I made.

Didn't take time to love her.

And it caused her love to fade.

Oh, if you have true love.

(If you have true love)

Take a tip from a man in misery.

Don't ever be lonely, a poor little fool like me.

Don't ever be lonely, a poor little fool like me

Oh, I see how much I was wrong.

To avoid such a love so true.

But now I really miss her.

And I see what loneliness can do.

Oh, if you have true love

(If you have true love)

Take a tip from a man in misery.

Oh, I wish I could turn back the time and

Have her back here with me.

I'd do anything to keep her

To avoid this pain and misery.

For those that are happy

(For those that's happy)

Take a tip from a man in misery.

Don't ever be lonely, a poor little fool like me.

Don't ever be lonely, a poor little fool like me.

(I beg you)

Don't ever be lonely

A poor little fool like me

(Oh, no, don't you

Ever be lonely)

Don't ever be lonely

A poor little fool like me

(I beg you)

Don't ever be lonely

A poor little fool like me

I wanted to share the lyrics of this song that I wrote in 1970. I did not like the thought of being alone or not having someone close in my life. I came from a big family, so I didn't have many occasions to be alone to myself. As an adult, I enjoyed the company of my wife and kids.

God will go through great lengths to bring His children back home. He is intentional and knows precisely how, when, and what He will do to get you to see that He is all you need.

In my case, He had to get me alone to help me focus on Him. I must say, He had been incredibly long-suffering with me. No matter how many opportunities came up with God calling me back to Him, I still had not made the ultimate decision that I needed to make the return. I hadn't surrendered my all to God the Father through Jesus Christ.

I was unaware, but God had planned the perfect set up to finally get me where He needed me to be. His plan was fool-proof.

After another intense argument, I struck my wife. This time, she had finally come to the end of her rope and left. I gave her a few days to cool off and then decided to call her to come back as I usually did. Only this time, I was not getting a response.

Everyone else had already moved out of the house, so I was alone. It was the perfect opportunity for God to get my full attention. Naturally, I did not want to accept that things were all that bad. I told myself, "I'm not completely alone; at least I have my dog here with me." Well, I guess God heard that and made another adjustment.

One morning, I went out to feed my dog and got a real shock instead. I found that my dog had popped the leash and ran away from home. I know it sounds like an old country song, but I swear it is the truth.

I stood there, scratching my head, and holding the broken dog strap that was still connected to the chain in my hand. I was wondering why in the world would my dog feel the need to run away.

I didn't give up hope though. I figured he would eventually make his way back to the house once he got hungry and tired from roaming the streets. Day after day, I checked to see if the dog came back to the yard. Let me tell you, that dog never came back! That was a sure sign that God wanted me to be entirely by myself.

No matter how much I tried to call and talk to my wife, I could not get Imer or the kids to talk to me. One day I picked up the phone to try to make a call, and I heard a recorded voice message saying, "Your phone has been disconnected..." The phone was in my daughter's name, and when she found out her mother and I had broken up, she thought I had moved on. She had the phone disconnected.

I drank myself to the point of drunkenness almost every night. I thought that maybe overdosing would be a sure way out of this rotten life I had made for myself. As I mentioned earlier, I thought of suicide multiple times, but I had only attempted it once, and this would be my second and final attempt.

The depression was so bad, and I was tired. I decided to put a drug and alcohol concoction together with the hope that I would go to sleep permanently. Well, it did not work. Instead of dying in my sleep, I woke the next morning feeling awful with a massive hangover.

Later that night, I decided to turn on the television to get my mind off my problems. I found myself watching this Christian channel called Trinity Broadcasting Network. The message preached at that time moved me so intently. I knew it was a message sent from God just for me. The Holy Spirit was using this minister to say exactly what my heart would receive and at just the right time.

I cannot remember the pastor's name, but at the end of the sermon, he said, "If anyone of you hearing this message would like to decide to come back to God right now, pick up the phone and call our prayer line and one of our counselors can pray with you."

I centered on those 4 words, COME BACK TO GOD. Wow! That's it! I could've always come back to God. That was always an option. It was the only option to save my life. I don't know why it took me so long to get that.

As I think about this now, I can't help but think about Dorothy in the Wizard of Oz. She wandered all over the city, following a yellow brick road and meeting crazy characters that were lost as she was. She had to deal with flying monkeys, lions, tigers, and bears. Not to mention running from a mean, shoe-loving witch. She could have skipped all of that messy drama and just clicked her heels three times to get back home.

Well, THANKFULLY I didn't need to click my heels, but what I did was grab that phone and dialed the prayer line number. I felt like this was my last chance for help. I poured my whole heart out unto this total stranger, and you know what? I did not care! I needed to be born again! I wanted to be free from the bondage that I was living in! I needed to be whole! I needed JESUS as my Lord and Savior, and this was all that mattered to me.

That counselor prayed one of the most anointed and powerful prayers with me, and for the first time, I felt the Spirit of God come over me in such an unusual and overwhelming way.

Sweet Surrender

I surrendered my life to Christ that night. I finally stopped running, and you know what else? I was so relieved! The peace I felt, WOW! I can hardly describe it! The scripture that comes to mind for me as I share this with you is from Psalms chapter 103 verses 1-5 from The Passion Translation

1 With my whole heart, with my whole life,

and with my innermost being,

I bow in wonder and love before you, the holy God!

2 Yahweh, you are my soul's celebration.

How could I ever forget the miracles of kindness

you've done for me?

3 You kissed my heart with forgiveness, in spite of all I've done.

You've healed me inside and out from every disease.

4 You've rescued me from hell and saved my life.

You've crowned me with love and mercy.

5 You satisfy my every desire with good things.

You've supercharged my life so that I soar again

like a flying eagle in the sky!

I highlighted verses 3 and 4 because these really added gravy to the
steak for me.

3 You kissed my heart with forgiveness, in spite of all I've done.

You've healed me inside and out from every disease.

4 You've rescued me from hell and saved my life.

You've crowned me with love and mercy.

What a loving Father! Even after all that I did to try to get away from him, God's love chased me down and pulled me up from the path of destruction. He forgave me, healed me, saved me, and then claimed me as His own with love and mercy. It's mind-blowing every time I think about it.

Immediately upon receiving Christ as Lord and Savior, we inherit these amazing benefits. You will never find a better benefits package than the one God gives those who make Him Lord.

Now that I was born-again, the first thing I did was find a Bible so I could start reading it. I specifically looked for all the letters in red because I wanted to read what Jesus had to say first. I was so excited about my long-awaited return back to the open arms of my God.

The next day, I went looking for a church where I could go to worship God and fellowship with other believers. I had not stepped foot in any place of worship for a while, so I knew I was changed. I was no longer the same person.

I remember praying to God and asking Him to remove all of those sinful desires from me and He did! Some things washed away instantly, while other things are still a work in progress. All I know is that God did major work in me and He is faithfully finishing the work He started.

I called Imer to tell her what had happened. I was hoping that she would believe me, but of course, she did not. She did not trust anything I had to say and I couldn't blame her.

In the past, I would always tell her anything I thought she wanted to hear to get her to come back home. This time I had to prove to her that I was for real. She needed to know that I was not the same man as before.

I continued to pray and seek God through His Word. I only watched Christian television programs and I was consistently going to church as well.

My sister Billie was one of the first persons to notice my transformation, and she told Imer that she saw a genuine change in me.

After three months of separation, I decided to make another phone call to talk to Imer. She allowed me to share my heart and the details of my transformation.

We spoke on the phone for hours, and she started to believe me. She knew I had never talked to her about such things. Shortly after that, we met up. I got Imer to start coming to church with me, and by God's grace, she was born-again and our marriage was restored.

Day by day, I was able to prove to her that I was not the same man and that God had indeed changed my heart. It felt so good to get my life back on track. If only I had come back to God sooner. I would've saved myself a whole lot of unnecessary pain.

CHAPTER 5
FOR SUCH A TIME AS THIS

I can say this repeatedly without shame! I am now a new man! The scripture that comes to mind is this one out of 2 Corinthians 5:17 "Therefore if anyone is in Christ, he is a new creation; old things have passed away behold all things have become new." AMEN! It is the real deal.

I will not say that everything is now a piece of cake for me. I would love to say that I am problem-free, but that is not the case. However, my response is better, and my outlook on life is better.

I'm no longer burdened by guilt or the meaningless effort of trying to be perfect. Now I commit to putting my life in God's hands each day He gives me. I know and understand who I am and Whose I am.

I always knew that my life was not by accident. At one time, I lost my identity, but I found my true identity in Jesus Christ. I fell in love with the Savior of the world. My focus has become centered on His love for me. All I want to do is make sure that I am showing Him every day how much I love and appreciate His sacrifice and faithfulness towards me.

After becoming born-again, things were looking up for me. Most of my family had welcomed me back into their lives, and my calling to live holy and set apart was very clear to me.

I had prayed to God to ask Him what work He would have me to do in His kingdom. I wanted to work for Him and serve in the body of Christ. I studied the Bible regularly to learn more about God and the plans He had for His people.

Shortly after my restored faith, I got some incredibly sad news. On November 7, 1991, my brother Carter suffered a heart attack and died. His death would be a very tough blow to the family. We all loved Carter and could not believe that he would die so soon. He was 53 years old.

He did not seem to have any significant health issues that I could remember. The tragedy of Carter's passing will always stay with me. I am so glad that we were on good terms before his passing.

I was on good terms with all my siblings at this time in our lives. Although Carter is no longer with us here on earth, he will always be in our hearts and our thoughts. I miss you, my little brother.

Restoration

My testimony may sound similar to a lot of people's testimony, but it is not the same. Just as our fingerprints may look somewhat the same, our distinct markings identify us and make us uniquely different.

I am sure that someone can identify with my struggles; I do understand that some people may not be able to relate to it. I can only trust that my story and my testimony are supposed to help someone out there somewhere to know that they can start over too.

Don't believe the negative thoughts telling you every reason why you aren't good enough or why God's grace will never work for you. These are some of the lies Satan wants you to believe. He will use your thoughts, your past, your fears, and anything possible to keep you from getting where you need to be.

Two consistent lies the devil will use against God's chosen people are these: "You have gone too far into the darkness to be saved" or "you have done too much wrong for God to accept you." Please don't believe either of those lies!

The Parable Of A Lost Son

One of my favorite Bible stories that Jesus himself shared was about the story of the father and the prodigal son. God knows how we think, and He knows the strategy of the enemy to keep us in bondage and away from Him. This parable that Jesus shared gives us a fundamental basis of how we can understand the Father's love and acceptance for us. I will share this reference from scripture.

11 Jesus continued: "There was a man who had two sons. 12 The younger one said to his father, 'Father, give me my share of the estate.' Therefore, he divided his property between them.

13 "Not long after that, the younger son got together all he had, set off for a distant country and there squandered his wealth in wild living. 14 After he had spent everything, there was a severe famine in that whole

country, and he began to be in need. 15 So he went and hired himself out to a citizen of that country, who sent him to his fields to feed pigs. 16 He longed to fill his stomach with the pods that the pigs were eating, but no one gave him anything.

17 "When he came to his senses, he said, 'How many of my father's hired servants have food to spare, and here I am starving to death! 18 I will set out and go back to my father and say to him: Father, I have sinned against heaven and you. 19 I am no longer worthy of being called your son; make me like one of your hired servants.' 20 So he got up and went to his father.

"But while he was still a long way off, his father saw him and was filled with compassion for him; he ran to his son, threw his arms around him and kissed him.

21 "The son said to him, 'Father, I have sinned against heaven and you. I am no longer worthy of being called your son.'

22 "But the father said to his servants, 'Quick! Bring the best robe and put it on him. Put a ring on his finger and sandals on his feet. 23 Bring the fattened calf and kill it. Let's have a feast and celebrate. 24 For this son of mine was dead and is alive again; he was lost and now found.' So they began to celebrate.

25 "Meanwhile, the older son was in the field. When he came near the house, he heard music and dancing. 26 So he called one of the servants and

asked him what was going on. 27 'Your brother has come,' he replied, 'and your father has killed the fattened calf because he has him back safe and sound.'

28 "The older brother became angry and refused to go in. So his father went out and pleaded with him. 29 But he answered his father, 'Look! All these years I've been slaving for you and never disobeyed your orders. Yet you never gave me even a young goat so I could celebrate with my friends. 30 But when this son of yours who has squandered your property with prostitutes comes home, you kill the fattened calf for him!'

31 "'My son,' the father said, 'you are always with me, and everything I have is yours. 32 But we had to celebrate and be glad because this brother of yours was dead and is alive again; he was lost and now is found.'"

I know God saved me for such a time as this. I was not supposed to keep this to myself, and I won't keep it to myself. If God gives me a new day, I want to use it to share His love and truth. We are to live as children of light. We are beaming with love and truth for the world to see. It is who Christ is, and it is who we must become.

Maybe you're not an entertainer like I was. You may be a maintenance worker, a teacher, a politician, a police officer, a homemaker, or a pastor that is tired of living an unfulfilled life. You could be anyone doing anything. You could know the truth or be clueless about who God is. What matters most to God the Father is that you come back to Him.

For years I kept myself from receiving the apparent solution to peace. If you're facing a problem bigger than you are, know that it's not bigger than God. He can fix it for you just like He did for me.

I was a cheater, abuser, blasphemer, drug, and alcohol user. I hid behind a mask, hoping no one would figure me out or see my pain. You may have some of those same demons oppressing you. No one else sees what's going on because you've learned how to hide it real good.

Can I let you in on something? God sees you! He knows what you're hiding from everyone else. Don't let these things keep getting control over you. Don't allow any more years of your life to be wasted by some of the same foolish mistakes I made.

If you know that this is for you, seek God for help. He will change your heart. All you need to do is ask Him to come into your heart and make Himself known to you. He is knocking on your door right now. Open up to him. Confess, repent, and turn from your sins.

From Entertainer To Pastor

Several people have made that transition from entertainer to a pastor. I know a few famous people are on that list, but I will not name them. All I know is that I did not think that I would be one of those transferees.

After years of attending different churches in our area, I begin to sense the Lord moving me into the calling of Pastor. I had been a deacon, choir member, and superintendent of the deacons in some of the churches I had attended.

I knew that I desired to study the role of a pastor. I decided to take some theology and correspondence courses to become a licensed minister of the gospel.

Becoming a minister was one of the most treasured achievements of my life. I worked hard and studied for that license. At the end of the course, I had to take my final exam. When I got my results and realized I had passed, I was ecstatic! I couldn't wait to get my official papers in the mail.

After a few days had gone by, I got a call from the director of the school. He said, "Mr. Cornelius, I wanted to call you to congratulate you on scoring the highest score of 100% on the final exam." My heart was so thrilled! It was not just about scoring 100%; it was about knowing that God was working in my life to bring me to this point. It was confirmation that I was in His will and on the right track.

I had now followed through with the first step of becoming an ordained minister. The next step was to pray and ask God for my assignment. I needed to know where to serve in ministry. I prayed and prayed until finally, God revealed to me that I would be serving as a pastor of my own church home.

I asked God to tell me what the name of the ministry should be. The name given to me was "Blood of the Lamb Ministries." After receiving the ministry name, I began to search for the location of the church building we could use.

After much prayer and searching, we found a storefront location in Hallandale, Florida, and 1995; we opened the doors to our new church home.

Blood Of The Lamb Ministries

Having a church of our own felt incredibly surreal. It was all new to us. Who would have thought that we would be starting and running our church? We had gained some experience from the other churches we attended, and with the help of God, we began to put all of the church affairs in order.

As expected, we were leading others to Christ through sharing His gospel, marrying couples, baptizing new believers, praying for the sick, christening the little ones as well as doing outreach work in the community.

My favorite part was seeing people come to the altar to receive Jesus Christ as their Lord and personal Savior.

We didn't have a vast congregation, nor did that matter to us. Our goal was to get people saved. God blessed us to bring several members to Christ. Once they heard the message of love through the gospel of Jesus Christ, the rest was easy. If Jesus is lifted high, He will draw all men unto Him. AMEN!

We obeyed the Lord and took on this challenge of running a church for a couple of years. However, music was still so much a part of who I was. I continued writing songs that came from my heart. The only change was that these songs were not about the people in my life or me. It was music about God and his incredible love for us.

I wanted to get these messages of God's love recorded so that more people would have the opportunity to hear them. I wanted to be a part of encouraging people through these songs.

After praying to the Lord, I followed my heart to produce my first gospel album called Positive Messages. I was able to pour my heart and soul into this project. It has all the songs I wrote during the first years of coming to know Christ as my Lord and Savior.

I enjoyed making this CD because it ministers to everyone. The message is about salvation, praise, and love for God. It makes me cry to think about the lyrics when I hear them in each song. Especially the song God Is Able.

I am a witness to God's mercy and His grace. I know what God can do because of what He did in my life. Thank you, Father God, Thank you so much!

Melodies From Heaven

As I was growing in my walk with the Lord, I found myself writing more and more songs to glorify Him. The gift to write from my heart is a part of who I am. It was not supposed to go away just because I became a Christian. God put the desire in my heart in the first place. Music is my best way of expression. I can write what I feel and share it with God and the entire world around me.

While sitting in my home studio, I realized that I still had so many songs written, but never recorded. After finishing my first gospel album and promoting it locally, I put another collection of songs together.

This time I wanted to do something a little more different from what I was used to doing. I even included a new (Christian) Version of my song Too Late To Turn Back Now." It was so much fun putting this one together. The CD's title is Positive Messages Volume 2 which was another compilation of praise and worship songs.

After much prayer and fasting, God revealed to me that the church formed under Blood of the Lamb Ministries was no longer going to be in a storefront location. That door would close, but another would open for ministry.

Blood of the Lamb Ministries would now be a traveling ministry, and I would function in the office of an evangelist.

Immediately I started to reach out to friends and former colleagues, letting them know that I would love to share my testimony and the music that I now do for the Lord. I began taking speaking engagements at other churches as well as performing in gospel concerts to promote and share my music ministry.

It was not so easy, transitioning, though. People would invite me to function with the hope that I would still sing the songs from back in the day. They were not always open to hearing me sing the gospel music I had prepared to sing. It is not that I have anything against those classic songs; I have a new message on my heart that I want to share.

Most of the organizations that booked me for an appearance understand that request. They had no problem with me singing my gospel songs if I agreed to sing some of my earlier hits with Cornelius Brothers and Sister Rose.

New Journey And Direction

Traveling is not a new concept for me. I had to go to different cities to do shows when I was part of CSBR. It is simply amazing how God will use the skills that we developed while living unsaved and then use them for His purposes when we are finally living our lives for Him.

In the early 2000s, I was getting around and going to different places for speaking engagements and singing. A close friend of mine had booked me at some events throughout my hometown area of South Florida. I was also getting calls to do bookings in North and South Carolina and some parts of Georgia.

I do not travel nearly as much as I did with the group back in the '70s, but I believe that the doors will open and that God will make room for my testimony to bring Him the honor and glory. That is why I am writing this book.

My priorities and my desires have changed entirely from when I was living the wild and crazy life I lead back in the day. I am determined to make pleasing God my number one priority. He, in return, gives me the wisdom and abilities to be my best in every area of my life. I know I am not perfect, but because of Him, I am a better Christian, husband, father, and overall person.

Most importantly, His Word declares that He will finish the work He started in me. God is not a man that He would lie. He is faithful to keep all of His promises. We can stand on His Word and know that He will come through.

CHAPTER 6
LESSONS I HAVE LEARNED

After 70 plus years on earth, you would hope to have gained some wisdom. Rumor has it that your gray hairs reflect that wisdom. I believe that I have enough gray hair to prove that I have learned my fair share of life lessons. I will gladly share some of those things in this chapter of the book.

For starters, I have learned that having a good life is more about the choices we make. If you want a hard and challenging life, here are some steps to take:

Avoid listening to sound wisdom and godly counsel, hang around negative people, do everything your way no matter what, be lazy, run from God as long as you can, and lastly, be sure to maintain a prideful, arrogant attitude. Over time, you will find that these choices will guarantee you a life of sheer misery.

On the other hand, if you want a life that is productive and fulfilling, full of God's peace, love, joy, goodness, and inherently more satisfying. You can obtain this type of life by doing the opposite of what I prescribed for a difficult life.

Our Father in heaven is the One who knows all things. He is the Almighty and All-knowing God. He wants us to learn everything we need to know about Him and how we can enjoy the benefits of being a child of God. One of those benefits is living an abundant life.

In John 10:10, Jesus said, "The thief does not come except to steal, and to kill, and to destroy." "I have come that they may have life and that they may have it more abundantly."

I know the thief in this text refers to the devil, but what does it mean to have an abundant life?

I decided to search the internet to see what I could find under the definition of "abundant life." I found a good description from Wikipedia that says this the term "abundant life" comes from the bible verse John 10:10, "I come that they might have life and that they might have it more abundantly." "More abundantly" means to have a superabundance of a thing. "Abundant life" refers to life in its abounding fullness of joy and strength for mind, body, and soul. "Abundant life" signifies a contrast to feelings of lack, emptiness, and dissatisfaction, and such feelings may motivate a person to seek for the meaning of life and a change in their life.

This is a good definition of abundant life; however, I found an even more excellent break down of how to live an abundant life straight from the book of Psalms chapter 1:

Psalm 1 CEB version

1 The truly happy person

doesn't follow wicked advice,

doesn't stand on the road of sinners,

and doesn't sit with the disrespectful.

2 Instead of doing those things,

these persons love the Lord's Instruction,

and they recite God's Instruction day and night!

3 They are like a tree replanted by streams of water,

which bears fruit at just the right time

and whose leaves don't fade.

Whatever they do succeeds.

4 That's not true for the wicked!

They are like dust that the wind blows away.

5 And that's why the wicked will have no standing in the court of justice—

Neither will sinners in the assembly of the righteous.

6 The Lord is intimately acquainted

with the way of the righteous,

but the way of the wicked is destroyed.

Making the best choices for our lives will give us more opportunities for steady growth and success. It is essential to know that the more we seek God's face and His ways, the more He will reveal himself to us. We will know His truth, we will know His plans, and we will know our part to play in His kingdom.

Everything That Glitters Isn't Gold

When I think about all that God has done for me, I can't help but feel joy in my heart. Having some fame, money, and material things do not mean anything if you do not have the peace of the Lord in your heart.

Look around and see what is going on. There is nothing new under the sun. People today have the same temptations we did back in our time and the times before that. The style and format are different, but the root of it all is quite the same.

The season of good times, partying, and spending loads of money on temporary things to feel better will fly by quicker than you think. I found out that I wasted so much valuable time and money, and my life was no better for it.

The fast times and rollercoaster lifestyle is in no way limited to entertainers. It is just as prevalent in the lives of the blue-collar, white-collar, and every collar. I am merely coming at this from my background as a former entertainer.

Because of my experiences in the entertainment industry, I do know it has great pull and power over the masses, and some use it overwhelmingly to distort, deceive, and distract the minds of people.

It's customary to chase after that big deal, branding of oneself, and the power that comes with that. It looks so appealing when you see all of these beautiful images of celebrities vacationing on the beach and posing in front of a brand-new Lamborghini. It's enticing for sure. However, I guarantee that only a handful of the million and one working artists in the world can afford that kind of luxury.

Here's the worst part of it. Some fame chasers are so desperate to sign to a record label, get a modeling contract or acting gig. They are willing to degrade and exploit themselves for it, even if it means promoting all sorts of evil and immoral acts to get it. Don't sell your soul for fool's gold!

Like a hamster on a wheel, you will never stop once you get on. It's a constant work of trying hard to stay relevant and not only get to the top but to stay on top. Now with all the social media outlets and everyone having such easy access, self-marketing and self-promoting are necessarily easier, yet it comes as a gamble.

As quickly as you are followed, viewed, or liked for several things you've done well if you say or post one wrong statement, you can cause a whirlwind of damage to your image. It's like the game of a coin toss, with one swift motion you can be at the head of the game or end up on the tail end of things hoping to make a comeback.

There are a lot of hidden agendas and fake bait out there luring those who are eager to catch a break or deal. The key is to know and understand the "big catch" is not all it's cracked up to be. It comes with a price. My advice is to consider the cost and make sure you can live comfortably with your decisions. Do not get involved or sign up for anything major without fully understanding the fine lines and the expectations.

Nothing is wrong with wanting to pursue your dream. Especially if you have the passion, talent, and desire to do so. I will stress to you that it is imperative to stay grounded, hold to your values, seek wise counsel, and have a sound support system of family and friends. If you are careful, you will beseech the advice of those who genuinely have your best interest at heart.

The <u>love of money</u> is the root of all sorts of evil. God knows we have needs, and He does give money and resources to help us live and take care of our needs, and some of our wants too. It is when money or material things become a god or an idol in our lives. These things can enslave us and drive us to do whatever it takes to keep its supply coming in. That is when things start to get dangerous.

God is clear in His Word when He says that we can't serve money and Him. We will have to choose between the two of whom we will serve. Just know that money will never be able to satisfy us completely.

Indeed money is valuable and necessary to accomplish practically everything in our daily living. However, cash is still a limited commodity. Only God has the power to give you complete satisfaction.

Besides that, God is not going to come in second place for your heart. He will step back and allow us to decide who or what will take the first place. Beware! When God is not first, get ready for a series of problems lined up at your door.

The Devil Will Offer Gifts Too

Yes, the devil will suggest things to us and even try harder to convince us that it is a blessing from God. However, think about what you are doing and ask yourself, "Would God be pleased with what I'm doing?" "Would God be honored by this?" If you answered no to those questions, then most likely, those are not gifts or opportunities from God. God's Word says:

17 Every good gift and every perfect gift is from heaven above and comes down from the Father of lights, with whom there is no variation or shadow of turning James 1:17.

Notice the clarifying of the words GOOD and PERFECT gift. Why is that? Because not every gift is good, perfect, or from God.

Satan, on the other hand, uses gifts and deceptive tactics to tempt us to go against God. In the end, we end up losing a lot more than what we had when we started.

The devil tried to tempt Jesus the Son of God with his unique set of "gifts" too, but Jesus was not surprised or caught off guard by the devil's schemes. He was prepared and knew He would have to experience this session of temptation before getting involved in His mission and ministry. Here is where the Bible refers to the temptation of Jesus. It is from Matthew chapter 4 verses 1-11.

Then Jesus was led by the Spirit into the wilderness to be tempted by the devil. 2 After fasting forty days and forty nights; he was hungry. 3 The tempter came to him and said, "If you are the Son of God, tell these stones to become bread."

4 Jesus answered, "It is written: 'Man shall not live on bread alone, but on every word that comes from the mouth of God. 5 Then the devil took him to the holy city and had him stand on the highest point of the temple. 6 "If you are the Son of God," he said, "throw yourself down. For it is written:" 'He will command his angels concerning you, and they will lift you in their hands so that you will not strike your foot against a stone.

7 Jesus answered him, "It is also written: 'Do not put the Lord your God to the test.

8 Again, the devil took him to a very high mountain and showed him all the kingdoms of the world and their splendor. 9 "All this I will give you," he said, "if you will bow down and worship me."

10 Jesus said to him, "Away from me, Satan! For it is written: 'Worship the Lord your God and serve him only.

11 Then the devil left him, and angels came and attended him.

The first thing offered to Jesus was the opportunity of self-indulgence through entitlement. The enemy knew that Jesus was weak from fasting and thought that using food to entice Him would be an easy one and done. Of course, he knew Jesus had the power to turn those stones into bread. Therefore, He tries to manipulate Him using what I call the "entitlement" trap. Listen, just because you can do certain things, does not mean that you should.

This trap is so common, and it gets most of us daily. Self- indulgence and entitlement is a sure way to go against the best that God has for you. Telling yourself things like "Well, I deserve this.", or "I'm quite capable of handling this my way!

We also can be impatient. So many of us do not want to go through the process of waiting for things. We want everything to happen in the right way. Our microwave minute society has trained us that we must get what we want quick, fast, and in a hurry.

When I was out on the road, away from my wife and family, I would steadily fall for the trap of self-indulgence. I could hear myself saying things like, "Well, I owe it to myself to have a good time.", or "Hey, this lifestyle is just part of the music business..."

In the scripture above, it also says the devil even offered Jesus the kingdoms of this world if Jesus would only worship him. That is a lot more than a Mercedes or a mansion, and yet Jesus rejected it because He knew this gift was not without a considerable price and sacrifice. He also knew that it was a trap to ruin God's plan of redemption and to stop God's mission of saving humanity from eternal damnation and separation.

Jesus did not hesitate to resist temptation via the Word of God. He not only quoted it, but He believed in it and stood on it. Do you know why? Because He is the WORD!

John.1 "[1] in the beginning was the Word, the Word was with God, and the Word was God. [2] The same was at the beginning with God. [3] All things were made by him, and without him was not anything made that was made."

He also knew the wickedness and real agenda of the devil. We too must stand on the Word of God. We need to have a healthy relationship with Him to know and stand on His Word instantly without hesitation or question. It is also important to understand what God wants for us. His holy spirit will help us to distinguish what is really from Him and what is a set up from the enemy.

Here is a more practical example. If a cashier accidentally gives you the wrong change in your favor and you discovered it, do you say, "Thank you God for giving me more money back!" or do you realize that it was not a blessing and immediately go and correct that mistake?

God does not have to short a cashier's money bank to bless you. He does not have to steal it either. The only blessing in the situation would be the cashier seeing your integrity and godly character in returning the money and potentially keeping him or her from getting in trouble with their store manager and maybe losing their job.

Let us go a little bit deeper. All of us can be tempted by something. It is a part of life. Yet, God says that even when we are tempted, He always provides a way out.

1 Corinthians 10:13 (NLT) reads, "The temptations in your life are no different from what others experience and God is faithful. He will not allow the temptation to be more than you can stand."

When God blesses His people, there is no sorrow attached to it. There is no guilt and no need for compromise on the Word of God or your moral standing. Proverbs 10:22 says, "The blessing of the Lord makes a person rich, and he adds no sorrow with it."

The gifts or opportunities offered through any other sources OUTSIDE of God's will or the purpose of our lives may look appealing and alluring, but it could cost us MAJORLY in the end. "What do you benefit if you gain the whole world but lose your soul?" (Mark 8:36)

Owning many material things does not guarantee happiness. At times, those very things can keep us in bondage and separate us from God. More importantly, why choose to invest our entire lives and focus on pursuing temporary pleasures vs. investing our efforts in securing eternal rewards? Always consider the source of all opportunities, gifts, and promises. Pray and ask God to reveal to you if the opportunity presented is from Him. He will show you if it is His will for your life.

Bad Choices Create Bad Consequences

Something else I've learned in my journey through life is that adverse consequences come from bad choices. Some people believe that once they do something terrible and then pray to God for forgiveness, they should not have to suffer through with the consequences.

Throughout my years of running from God, I have suffered some consequences that have caused me much pain and regret. I have learned to accept that I can't change the past; I can only do my best to make things right going forward.

An excellent example in the Bible of suffering consequences from bad decisions is in the story about King David.

King David, as many of us know, achieved several great successes for the glory of God. As a young man, he slew a giant with a slingshot and a stone. He then joined the army and killed off many of the enemies of Israel during the war, he brought the Ark of the Covenant back to Israel, and he was a gifted musician and songwriter. We can thank him for most of the book of Psalms.

David accomplished quite a lot of good things during his lifetime, but in reading some of his stories, we also see that David messed up as well. One of the most famous of his mistakes was the one regarding a married woman named Bathsheba.

Bathsheba was married to an honorable man named Uriah. He was a soldier in King David's army. Uriah was a loyal and dedicated soldier. I am sure he was a stand out in his group, an active leader in the making. Most of all, he had great respect and admiration for King David and his country.

Well, as the story goes, King David was a warrior; he had been in many battles and enjoyed the thrill of killing the enemy. However, on this occasion, David decided to stay behind and NOT join his soldiers in this particular battle. This was poor choice #1.

During this time in history, it was prevalent for the kings to be directly involved in fighting wars on the battlefield with the troops. Of course, they were not usually on the front line, but somewhere in a proper position to lead their army into victory. I will share the Bible verse as a reference. It is from 2 Samuel 11:1

V.1 "In the spring, at the time when kings go off to war, David sent Joab out with the king's men and the entire Israelite army. They destroyed the Ammonites and besieged Rabbah. However, David remained in Jerusalem"

As you see from the text, King David had a responsibility to go off to war, but he declined. Instead, he sent his general to go on to battle without him.

There was no indication in the text that suggested David was in poor health or that he was old to disqualify him from fighting in combat. If that were so, then it would make sense. This was not the case.

What makes more sense to me is that David was becoming more of a lousy boss instead of a good leader. He used his position of authority irresponsibly and allowed himself to slip into a trap. He chose self-gratification over choosing integrity and displaying good character.

The story continues. King David was roaming about the halls (no doubt bored senseless.) As he walked around the roof of his palace, he looked down and noticed a beautiful woman bathing in her home. This happened to be a married woman named Bathsheba. He summoned some of his staff to bring her to him. This was poor choice#2.

Now once the staff brought her to King David, he took her into his private abode; they proceeded to have sexual intercourse. This would be poor choice#3.

Now after some time, Bathsheba discovers that she is pregnant by King David. She notifies him of her discovery, and David immediately starts deliberating over what he should do. He did not want to bring shame to her or himself. David decides to come up with a deceitful plan that he hopes will resolve things.

The plan was to summon Uriah back home from the battlefield so that he would sleep with his wife. That way, he would assume that he is the natural father of the baby. This would be poor choice #4.

Uriah, being the honorable soldier that he was, felt it is a disgrace to take time off while the rest of his fellow troops were in battle. Wow! Uriah had the conviction to do the right thing by the army of Israel more than the king himself did!

So, Uriah did not sleep with his wife but instead went back to finish the battle he started. Once King David's deceptive plan failed, he became desperate and decided to take extreme measures to cover up his mess.

Now we are at poor choice #5. David summons the general of his army and tells him to make sure to put Uriah in the line of fire when they are in a heated area of battle.

He planned to have Uriah killed so that he could legally take Bathsheba to be his wife and avoid disgrace. David thought that he cleverly covered up his actions and could go on living happily ever after. However, that would not be the last case. It does not matter what we may be able to hide from other people. God sees everything! David discovers this to be true when God sends his prophet Nathan to visit him after he and Bathsheba are married.

Here's the scripture found in 2 Samuel Chapter 12:1-22 (GWT)

The Lord sent Nathan to David. Nathan came to him and said, "There were two men in a particular city. One was rich, and the other was poor. 2 The rich man had a considerable number of sheep and cows, 3 but the poor man had only one little female lamb that he had bought. He raised her, and she grew up in his home with his children. She would eat his food and drink from his cup. She rested in his arms and was like a daughter.

4 "Now, a visitor came to the rich man. The rich man thought it would be a pity to take one of his sheep or cattle to prepare a meal for the traveler. So, he took the poor man's lamb and prepared her for the traveler."

5 David burned with anger against the man. "I solemnly swear, as the Lord lives," he said to Nathan, "the man who did this certainly deserves to die! 6 And he must pay back four times the price of the lamb because he did this and had no pity."

7 "You are the man!" Nathan told David. "This is what the Lord God of Israel says: I anointed you king over Israel and rescued you from Saul. 8 I gave you your master Saul's house and his wives. I gave you the house of Israel and Judah, and if this were not enough, I would have given you even more. 9 Why did you despise my word by doing what I considered evil? You had Uriah the Hittite killed in battle. You took his wife as your wife. You used the Ammonites to kill him. 10 So warfare will never leave your house because you despised me and took the wife of Uriah the Hittite to be your wife.

11 "This is what the Lord says: I will stir up trouble against you within your household, and before your own eyes, I will take your wives and give them to someone close to you. He will go to bed with your wives in broad daylight. 12 You did this secretly, but I will make this happen in broad daylight in front of all Israel."

13 Then David said to Nathan, "I have sinned against the Lord."

Nathan replied, "The Lord has taken away your sin; you will not die. 14 But since you have shown total contempt for the Lord by this affair, the son that is born to you must die." 15 Then Nathan went home.

The Lord struck the child that Uriah's wife had given birth to for David so that the child became sick. 16 David pleaded with God for the child; he fasted and lay on the ground all night. 17 The older leaders in his palace stood beside him to raise him from the ground, but he was unwilling, and he would not eat with them.

18 On the seventh day, the child died. However, David's officials were afraid to tell him that the child was dead. They thought, "While the child was alive, we talked to him, and he wouldn't listen to us. How can we tell him the child is dead? He may harm himself."

19, when David saw that his officials were whispering to one another, he realized that the child was dead. "Is the child dead?" David asked them.

"Yes, he is dead," they answered.

20 David got up from the ground, bathed, anointed himself, and changed his clothes. He went into the Lord's house and worshiped. Then he went home and asked for food. They placed food in front of him, and he ate.

21 His officials asked him, "Why are you acting this way? You fasted and cried over the child when he was alive. But as soon as the child died, you got up and ate."

22 David answered, "As long as the child was alive, I fasted and cried. I thought, 'Who knows? The Lord may be gracious to me and let the child live.' 23 why should I fast now that he is dead? Can I bring him back? Someday I'll go to him, but he won't come back to me."

He repented, and God indeed forgave him, but the terrible consequences for his poor choices were still in effect. Like David, we all have made or will make bad choices from time to time in our lives. The good news is that the closer we connect with God, making bad decisions will become less frequent. We eventually learn to discern and walk in the ways of Christ. It's like a baby learning how to walk in the natural. We must learn how to walk spiritually in the ways of Jesus.

It takes time, but it is not without some stumbles and falls. Thankfully, we have a heavenly Father who loves us so much. He will pick us up again, no matter how many times we fall. John 1:9 NIV says "if we confess our sins, he is faithful and just and will forgive us our sins and purify us from all unrighteousness."

As you may know, the story did not wholly end there for David. He and Bathsheba were able to conceive another son who became the next king of Israel, and he was King Solomon. God continued to show David's favor and mercy throughout the rest of his days as king. Most of all, God kept his promise to keep the family line of David seated on the throne, which now forever continues through Jesus Christ, the Messiah.

Take It From Me

Some people do not live long enough to tell their stories. They aren't able to tell you what they've learned from their past mistakes. If some could come back from the dead for just one day, maybe they would try to warn everyone around them about the dangers of chasing money, fame, and sinful pleasures. They might let us know that those things do not equate to a "good life." Here is a news flash! They are not coming back to tell us anything and that's okay!

I encourage you to listen to the voice of someone still here who made the mistake of chasing the counterfeit "good life." I can tell you firsthand that it is not worth losing your life for. More importantly, it's not worth your soul.

You have people from all lifestyles committing suicide from depression or dying from alcoholism and drug overdoses every day. They're not free and they're not living in peace. This is a good reason to rethink what should be most relevant to all of us. I can tell you what it is for me and it can be for you too. It is allowing the God who made us and loves us so much, to show us how to live in His perfect peach and freedom.

Be free from the lies that you aren't loved or good enough. Be free from feeling that you have to please everyone by doing things God never intended for you to do. Be open to find your God-given purpose and fulfill that purpose with God's help.

Live free in knowing that money can't buy true riches like love, joy, peace, favor, healing, etc. Know that in Christ, you have access to all of His glorious true riches.

Our freedom costs God severely, but I know He would do it all over again because of His overwhelming love for us. Don't deny or waste this gift! Use it for all its intended purposes. This is how we can live an authentic good life.

My testimony is simply the work of God. I share it with the hope that people would take heed and learn from my experiences. I believe that I shorted myself from accomplishing a lot more because of my poor choices in the past. Still, I am grateful that my life did not end sooner before I came back to my Father God.

What is so good about God Most High, is that He can still restore us from the years that were lost. You may not be a young person physically again, but God can restore your strength and help you to accomplish things in your life at this moment and time.

If you are young and feel like you want to "live it up" and party hard during your youthful days, I encourage you, don't gamble with your life and your eternity.

You never know what lies ahead of you in the path that you're on. If you are not following Christ, you are susceptible to unseen dangers you can't even begin to imagine.

Most of all, to die without Jesus Christ as your Lord and Savior will seal your fate for an eternity outside of God's eternal peace and presence.

It is crucial to gain the understanding that ETERNITY is never-ending. Anyone not accepting the gift of salvation through Jesus Christ will be cast into hell and live in torment and darkness forever. It's not God's choice to send anyone there; it's our free will to decide if we want to go there.

My life is much better than before because of what I know now. God is my captain. He guides me, and He orders my steps. I will not say that everything is perfect and that I don't have my fair share of problems, issues, or challenges in life. What I will say is that I wouldn't trade the life I now have, knowing and living for God; for the life, I had back then not knowing and living for God.

I prefer to go through life with Him as my anchor and light than to struggle through the world alone.

The Lord is blessing me every day in so many ways. LET HIM DO THE SAME FOR YOU.

Do Not Wait Until It Is Too Late!

I know I mentioned throughout this book, including in the title of this book, that it is not too late to turn back. That is only true for those of us who are living and breathing at this very moment.

Unfortunately, the moment we stop breathing, it does become too late. As of now, there is no cure for physical death. For all of us who are born into this world, there is also an appointed time to die. As a believer in Christ, I have an eternal hope that gives me peace about death and eternity. I know to be absent from the body is to be present with the Lord, and it will be a glorious event when I see my Savior face to face.

I also believe we are living in the last days. I know that some people may not want to consider this, but the Bible speaks on this very clearly. 2Timothy3 v1-5

"But mark this: There will be terrible times in the last days. 2 People will be lovers of themselves, lovers of money, boastful, proud, abusive, disobedient to their parents, ungrateful, unholy, 3 without love, unforgiving, slanderous, without self-control, brutal, not lovers of the good, 4 treacherous, rash, conceited, lovers of pleasure rather than lovers of God— 5 having a form of godliness but denying its power. Have nothing to do with such people."

We can't afford to close our eyes to the things that may be hard to digest. It is relevant, and it is necessary to know that truth. I believe in what 2 Timothy 3:16 says:

16 All Scripture is God-breathed and is useful for teaching, rebuking, correcting, and training in righteousness, 17 so that the servant of God[a] may be thoroughly equipped for every good work.

Some may say you can have a forever home here on earth, but there is no such thing. It may be a long-term home to raise your family, but our forever home will be in the eternal place we have chosen for our souls to live. This will be either in heaven or in hell.

When you read the book of Revelations in the Bible, it gives you a good description of both. I pray you will make the best choice. I know that I have.

If this book has helped you in any way, praise the Most High God! If you need prayer or you are struggling with suicidal thoughts, please be sure to check out the last page of this book.

It has helpful contact information, including the ministries I reached out to for prayer and support. Pray, read the Bible, and ask God to lead you to a Bible-teaching church to help you learn and grow in faith. I pray Jehovah God blesses you. Thanks for letting me share my story with you.

Ministry Resources

TBN 24-Hour Prayer Line:

Toll-free:1-888-731-1000

International (714)-731-1000

700 Club Prayer Line:

1-800-700-7000

Contact Information for Eddie L. Cornelius

Facebook.com/bloodofthelambministries

Great Book!,
albert 12/20

Made in the USA
Monee, IL
11 August 2020